**THE BOOK OF ART** is designed as an introduction to the visual arts: painting, drawing and sculpture. It provides a comprehensive survey, in ten volumes, of one of the most creative aspects of human effort, especially organized for the reader who does not have an extensive knowledge of the history of art.

Textual material prepared by experts in each school of art presents a detailed background of information. But, since art must be seen to be understood and appreciated, the essence of each volume lies in the color plates and the large number of black-and-white illustrations.

The first volume discusses the origins of the visual arts in the western world. The following five volumes are devoted to national schools of painting, extending roughly from the early Renaissance up to the mid-19th century. The two succeeding volumes cut across national divisions and deal first with the Impressionists and Post-Impressionists and then with 20th-century art. The ninth volume deals with the rich art of China and Japan.

The final volume, *How to Look at Art*, is designed to aid the reader in developing an appreciative understanding of the entire field of art. It discusses art of all schools and periods, with relevant illustrations, both in color and black-and-white, throughout the text. The same volume concludes with an illustrated glossary of art terms and a comprehensive index covering all ten volumes.

# THE BOOK OF ART

A Pictorial Encyclopedia of Painting, Drawing, and Sculpture

1 ORIGINS OF WESTERN ART
2 ITALIAN ART TO 1850
3 FLEMISH AND DUTCH ART
4 GERMAN AND SPANISH ART TO 1900
5 FRENCH ART FROM 1350 TO 1850
6 BRITISH AND NORTH AMERICAN ART TO 1900
7 IMPRESSIONISTS AND POST-IMPRESSIONISTS
8 MODERN ART
9 CHINESE AND JAPANESE ART
10 HOW TO LOOK AT ART

VOLUME 1

# ORIGINS OF WESTERN ART

# THE BOOK OF ART

A Pictorial Encyclopedia of Painting, Drawing, and Sculpture

# ORIGINS OF WESTERN ART

General Introduction by Sir Herbert Read

Text by Dr. Donald E. Strong

*Assistant Keeper, Department of Greek and Roman Antiquities, British Museum, London.*

Professor Giuseppe Bovini

*Director of the Institute of Antiquities, Ravenna, University of Bologna, Italy.*

Professor David Talbot Rice

*Watson Gordon, Professor of History of Art, Edinburgh University.*

Peter Lasko

*Assistant Keeper, Department of British and Medieval Art, British Museum, London.*

Professor G. Zarnecki

*Professor of History of Art and Deputy Director of the Courtauld Institute of Art, University of London.*

Dr. George Henderson

*Lecturer in History of Art, Manchester University.*



Grolier
INCORPORATED
NEW YORK MONTREAL MEXICO CITY SYDNEY

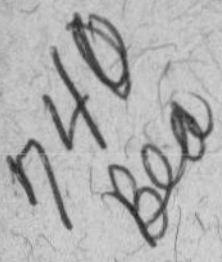


## NOTE TO THE READER

This volume, the first in the series, opens with Sir Herbert Read's General Introduction to the series as a whole, and then proceeds to outline the origins of Western Art in six chapters, each written by an authority in his particular field and each profusely illustrated in color and monochrome.

With the exception of this volume, and of the volumes entitled *Chinese and Japanese Art* and *How to Look at Art*, which are more general in their scope and treatment, each of the books in the series is arranged in accordance with the following basic plan:

First, a historical introduction sets out the main lines of development within the period covered, with special reference to the major artists and the major works of art. This is followed by an illustrated biographical section outlining the life and work of every major artist and important minor artist. Next follow sections of Color Plates, Drawings, and Sculpture. A final section, entitled Influences and Developments, rounds off the volume by drawing together the main ideas and characteristics of schools and styles, and by exploring the internal and external influences that have made their impact on the development of the arts during the period concerned.

Throughout the series the location of every work of art is included in its caption. Every effort has been made to include also the size, medium, and date of each work represented in the plates. The reader will appreciate that the precise dating of some works of art is the subject of scholarly controversy; however, no dates have been included here unless they have the authority of qualified experts and art historians.

A list of basic reference books for further reading appears on page 15.

To avoid repetitive explanation of basic technical terms, an illustrated Glossary is provided in the volume entitled *How to Look at Art*. Also in that volume is an Index listing every artist mentioned throughout the series.

NOTE – The terminal dates in the titles of some of the volumes are inevitably approximate. One volume will sometimes overlap with another. Some artists mentioned under French Art, for example, are also represented under the Impressionists, and the Post-Impressionists merge imperceptibly with the Moderns. In the ever-continuous process of Art it is difficult to contain schools or periods within precise boundaries.


First published 1965. Second Impression 1966. Third Impression 1967. Fourth Impression 1967.
Library of Congress Catalog Card Number: 65-10350

Designed and produced by George Rainbird Ltd., London
PRINTED IN ITALY by Amilcare Pizzi S.p.A., Milan

# General Introduction

## by Sir Herbert Read

Almost anyone who is asked to give an example of a work of art will answer with a painting, and in the Western World it would generally be a post-Renaissance European painting. There may be no logical defence of such an instinctive reaction; but it must to some extent determine the approach to any history of art. Even if it is the duty of the art historian and critic to correct this bias, it must be done tactfully or otherwise the potential reader will be lost.

There are, however, some good historical and psychological reasons for this public prejudice. To take the psychological reasons first. Though art is a term which includes all the fine arts—poetry and music as well as architecture, painting, engraving, and sculpture–it is the visual aspects of art that most directly affect our lives, for they are with us always and are part of our environment. Music and poetry are private arts, and need a deliberate approach on the part of their audiences. They are not physically present as objects, but must work invisibly on our sensibility. It is not a question of the relative importance of the arts—who can say that Raphael or Cézanne is 'more important than' Shakespeare or Mozart? It is merely a question of accessibility.

It is a also a question of sensuous impact. The eye may not be more sensitive, or more biologically essential, than the ear, but except in sleep it is working all the time; whereas we hear something or read something only occasionally or intermittently, and more effort is demanded to isolate the faculties needed for listening to music or reading poetry. There is, of course, a common disregard of the effort or attention necessary for looking at a work of visual art, and that is why the volume entitled *How to Look at Art* has been included in the series. But nevertheless, we are, so to speak, more easily available to visual impressions than to other kinds.

Historically the visual arts also have a certain priority. Prehistoric painting and sculpture are still a visual reality and we do not know of any other arts of such antiquity. Music was one of the arts of classical times, but it is still an art that is largely unknown to us, or only accessible to scholarly research. It is true that the art of painting survives from the Greek and Roman periods in fragments only, but these fragments are sufficient to establish a visual relationship with later periods, and sculpture and architecture help to establish the canons of all the visual arts of the period.

We speak of the Dark Ages and imagine a period when the visual chain was broken. But as will be seen from this first volume, devoted to the *Origins of Western Art*, there was no absolute hiatus in the visual tradition. Even if the personal continuity of master and pupil was broken from time to time, the visible monuments survived and provided inspiration from generation to generation. It is not only psychologically improbable but historically false to imagine periods of non-art: the evidence is on and in the earth and archaeologists every year make it more plentiful.

One of the main purposes, therefore, of an enterprise like the present one is to establish the historical continuity of one of man's most essential activities, and to do this by the most vivid means. Also by the most human means. There is no intention to establish a hierarchy among the visual arts, but painting and sculpture, as distinct from architecture and the applied arts, are more directly concerned with our human destiny—with men and women in their existential situation facing God or the Unknown, establishing relations between individuals and between societies, reconciling love and hate, life and death, earthly existence and spiritual immortality. Poetry and music have the same concern, but they do not, as I have already said, have the same immediacy. Only painting and sculpture (and sculpture in alliance with architecture) can encompass the whole destiny of mankind in visual images accessible to all mankind. For this reason the cathedrals of the Middle Ages, replete with all manner of visual images, were called the Bibles of the illiterate—which, in the 6th century, meant almost everybody.

The poor are no longer illiterate, but our prejudices in art remain pictorial, and in practice a convenient distinction is drawn between art and archaeology. This is our justification for not tracing the history of Western art back to its origins in the ancient civilizations of the Near East and Greece. No student of art would admit for a moment that these civilizations can be excluded from a general history of art, but our purpose in this enterprise has been more limited—namely, to relate the history of Western art (in which term we include American art) from the time it becomes a distinct tradition, which roughly speaking is the period corresponding to the Christian era. We have included a volume on the art of the Far East covering the same period because Oriental art has often exercised an influence on European art—for example, in Volume I mention is made of the influence of Oriental embroidered silks on the arabesque borders of the 11th-century frescoes in San Clemente, Rome, and the very word "arabesque" is an acknowledgment of this kind of influence. But equally it is a word for decorative rather than essential elements in a composition, and it must be admitted that the gulf separating the pictorial art of China or the sculpture of medieval India from the art of the West was never crossed by any but the most slender and perishable bridges. Chinese painting in particular remains to this day an art whose aesthetic principles are impenetrable to the people of the West.

It would be interesting to speculate on the reasons for this incompatibility of vision, but it relates to the religious and metaphysical foundations of the two cultures and any generalizations are bound to be too superficial. Completely different, even opposed, world visions are involved, and these have determined completely separate historical developments. Materialistic factors, of climate, race, and social economy, explain the superficial features of the contrast, but the metaphysical roots lie deeper, and are virtually inexplicable.

These considerations apply *a fortiori* to certain other civilizations which, until recently and then only in a superficial and eclectic manner, have not impinged on the European tradition in the visual arts. This is obviously true of the Pre-Columbian art of America, and of the arts of Africa and Polynesia, which have only entered into our artistic consciousness in the past hundred years. The influence of African sculpture on Cubism was direct and decisive, but it was a formal influence of short duration and quickly absorbed into the general development of modern art. The same observation can be made about Mexican sculpture: it provided certain stylistic motifs for individual artists like Henry Moore, but it did not permanently affect the general evolution of European art.

Confining ourselves to the Western tradition we find complications enough to challenge any attempt at a synoptic vision. There have been many attempts by individuals to write a general history of European art, but I know of no such work that does not suffer from the bias of an individual point of view, of a personal temperament or an inevitable prejudice. Even if it were possible for one scholar to have an adequate knowledge of the works of art created throughout the many centuries involved, to hold them in a steady focus would be beyond his mental powers. We are condemned to specialize, in art as in science, and the value of a cooperative enterprise like this is that the history and appreciation of each period is entrusted to a specialist. What the editors have done is so to plan the series that a balance is preserved, both as to extent and treatment, between the different parts or volumes into which this history has been divided.

It may seem to some readers that we have nevertheless betrayed our prejudices. Relatively more space is given to the last hundred years than to the Medieval period or even the Renaissance. This can be justified on the grounds that any historical perspective of so great a range inevitably recedes from the present, like the view from the wider end of a telescope. Not only do we know more about the immediate past; it is also more significant for us. We are relatively unmoved by Prehistoric art, and the pictorial elements in Greek and Roman art have not survived in sufficient quantity to impress us. With Medieval or Renaissance art we begin to feel at home; and when we come to modern art (by which we do not necessarily mean contemporary art), then we find ourselves involved both emotionally and ideologically in quite a distinct and deeper manner. Delacroix and Turner, Cézanne and van Gogh, Picasso and Paul Klee—these painters mean more to the average educated man, the unspecialized public, than even Giotto or Raphael, and certainly far more than any anonymous artist of the Middle Ages or Antiquity. We do not approach art with innocent eyes (alas!); we approach it with a vision and an intelligence conditioned by a thousand factors in our historical situation, and to ignore this limitation is pedantry.

Nevertheless, the present demands a knowledge of the past. We cannot understand or appreciate the beauty and vitality of modern art unless we understand and appreciate the long tradition that has brought it to its present situation and made it exactly what it is—any more than we can understand and appreciate the character and destiny of a nation unless we are familiar with its past history and basic traditions. We divide art into styles and periods just as we divide history into social groups and political movements, but the transitions are piecemeal and imperceptible in both, and the present grows from the past as organically as any vital process in nature. The Latin adage is more effective if we reverse it: *species mille, ars una*, which we might then translate: diversity is the soul of art.

I should perhaps add a word or two about the editorial procedure that brought this series into existence. The editorial committee planned the series and, within the limits set by the publishers, divided the subject into appropriate sections. Within the framework devised, they allowed each author or volume editor as much liberty as possible, and confined their criticisms to questions of length, proportion, and arrangement. The result, we believe, possesses both interest and vitality, and cannot fail to give the general reader a ready access to a vast and complicated subject. We have not asked our authors to simplify their texts unduly, for we believe that the subject demands and deserves a little effort on the reader's part. We believe that the facts presented are accurate and allow the reader to acquire a sufficiently comprehensive knowledge of the subject while not deadening his sensibility to the beauty and significance of the works of art illustrated and described. At the same time the series has been planned for permanent reference and educational guidance. Our task will have been successful if it leads to a desire for further knowledge and ever greater enjoyment.

# ORIGINS OF WESTERN ART

# Contents



## LIST OF COLOR PLATES

# ACKNOWLEDGMENTS

The publishers and producers wish to express their gratitude to all the museums, art galleries, collectors, photographers, and agencies who have courteously assisted them in obtaining the material for the illustrations reproduced in this volume.
They would especially like to thank the following:

The late Mr. G. W. Allen
Ampliaciones y Reproducciones Mas, Barcelona
Anderson, Rome
Antikvarisk-Topografiska Arkivet, Stockholm
Mr. P. de Antonis, Rome
Archives Photographiques, Paris
The Bavarian National Museum, Munich
Bayerische Staatsbibliothek, Munich
Bibliothèque Nationale, Paris
Bildarchiv Foto Marburg, Marburg an der Lahn
The Bodleian Library, Oxford
The Trustees of the British Museum, London
Buch-Kunstverlag, Ettal, Germany
Ets. J. E. Bulloz, Paris
Mr. Italo Buzzacchi, Rome
Caisse Nationale des Monuments Historiques, Paris
Mr. Peter Cannon Brookes, Birmingham, England
The Cathedral Treasury, Aachen
Mr. John Champion, Salisbury, England
The Right Reverend the Lord Bishop of Chichester, England
The City Museum, Liverpool, England
The Cleveland Museum of Art, Ohio
Corpus Christi College Library, Cambridge, England
The Courtauld Institute of Art, University of London
The Dean and Chapter of the Cathedral, Durham, England
Mr. W. L. Entwistle, Canterbury, England
Mr. Derek Evans, Hereford, England
Mr. Otto Fein, The Warburg Institute, London
The Syndics of the Fitzwilliam Museum, Cambridge, England
R. B. Fleming and Co. Ltd., London
Foto-Samhaber, Aschaffenburg, Germany
Fototeca de Architettura e Topografia dell'Italia Antica, Rome
Fototeca Catacombe di Priscilla, Rome
Fototeca Unione, Rome
Fratelli Alinari, S. A. (I.D.E.A.), Florence
John R. Freeman and Co. Ltd., London
Gabinetto Fotografico Nazionale, Rome
The German Archaeological Institute, Rome
Green Studio Ltd., Dublin
Herzog Anton Ulrich-Museum, Brunswick
Hessische Landes-und-Hochschulbibliothek, Darmstadt
Mr. Peter Heywood, Southwell, England
Hirmer Photoarchiv, Munich
Mr. Karel Just, London
The Warden and Fellows of Keble College, Oxford
Mr. A. F. Kersting, London
Kunsthistorisches Museum, Vienna
Lambeth Palace Library, London
Landesbibliothek, Darmstadt
Mr. J. A. Lavaud, Paris
The Lord Chamberlain's Office, London
The Mansell Collection, London
The Museum of Archaeology and Ethnology, Cambridge, England
National Buildings Record, London
The National Museum, Athens
Novosti Press Agency, Moscow
The Rev. A. F. Osbourne, Bradford-on-Avon, England
Mr. Pericles Papahadjidakis, Athens
Photographie Giraudon, Paris
The Pierpont Morgan Library, New York
Amilcare Pizzi S.p.A., Milan
Pontificia Commissione di Archeologia Sacra, Rome
Miss Josephine Powell, Rome
The Royal Collection, London, by gracious permission of Her Majesty the Queen
The Russell Trust Expedition
Rustington Cameras Ltd., Rustington England
Mr. Joseph Rykwert, London
Mr. Oscar Savio, Rome
Scala Istituto Fotografico Editoriale, Florence
Schnütgen Museum, Cologne
Schweizerisches Landesmuseum, Zurich
The Scottish Tourist Board, Edinburgh
Stearn and Sons, Cambridge, England
Thames and Hudson Ltd., London
Mr. Thörnig, Trier, Germany
Trinity College Library, Cambridge, England
The University of Chicago, Oriental Institute
The University Library, Utrecht
University of London Library
The Vatican Gallery, Rome
The Vatican Library, Rome
The Victoria and Albert Museum (Crown Copyright), London
The Warburg Institute, University of London
Mr. F. E. de Wilde, Oegstgeest, Holland
Woodmansterne Ltd., Watford, England
The Yugoslav Embassy, London
Professor G. Zarnecki, London

# ABBREVIATIONS

| | |
|---|---|
| Bibl. | Biblioteca, Bibliothèque |
| B.M. | British Museum, London |
| Cod. | Codex |
| Coll. | Collection |
| f. | folio |
| Fr. | French |
| Grec. | Greek |
| Hochschulbibl. | Hochschulbibliothek |
| in. | inches |
| Lat. | Latin |
| MS. | Manuscript |
| Mus. | Museo, Museum |
| Nat. | Nationale |
| Naz. | Nazionale |
| p. | page |
| r. | recto |
| S. | San, Santa |
| St. | Saint |
| Staatsbibl. | Staatsbibliothek |
| Ste. | Sainte |
| v. | verso |
| V. and A. | Victoria and Albert Museum, London |

# SOME BOOKS FOR FURTHER READING


CHAPTER 1: IMPERIAL ROMAN ART

G. M. A. Richter, *A Handbook of Greek Art*, New York and London, 1959.
A. Maiuri, *Roman Painting*, Geneva, 1963.
Donald E. Strong, *Roman Imperial Sculpture*, New York and London, 1961.
Mortimer Wheeler, *Roman Art and Architecture*, New York and London, 1964.
G. M. A. Hanfmann, *Roman Art*, New York and London, 1964.
J. D. Beazley and B. Ashmole, *Greek Sculpture and Painting to the End of the Hellenistic Period*, Cambridge, England, 1965.

CHAPTER 2: EARLY CHRISTIAN ART

C. R. Morey, *Early Christian Art*, Princeton, 1942.
David Talbot Rice, *The Beginning of Christian Art*, New York and London, 1957.
Giovanni Bovini, *Ravenna Mosaics*, New York and London, 1957.

CHAPTER 3: THE EASTERN ROMAN EMPIRE

J. H. Breasted, *Oriental Forerunners of Byzantine Painting*, Chicago, 1924.
E. W. Anthony, *A History of Mosaics*, Boston, 1935.
David Talbot Rice, *The Art of Byzantium*, New York and London, 1959; *Art of the Byzantine Era*, New York and London, 1963.
John Beckwith, *The Art of Constantinople*, London, 1961.
René Huyghe (editor), *Encyclopedia of Byzantine and Medieval Art*, New York and London, 1963.

CHAPTER 4: WESTERN EUROPE TO THE 11TH CENTURY

Roger Hinks, *Carolingian Art*, London, 1935.
David Talbot Rice, *English Art 871-1100*, Oxford, 1952.
Margaret Rickert, *Painting in Britain: The Middle Ages*, (Pelican History Art) London, 1954.
E. Kitzinger, *Early Medieval Art in the British Museum*, London, 1955.
André Grabar and Carl Nordenfalk, *Early Medieval Painting*, Geneva, 1957.

CHAPTER 5: ROMANESQUE ART

E. W. Anthony, *Romanesque Frescoes*, Princeton, 1951.
George Zarnecki, *English Romanesque Sculpture*, London, 1951; *Later English Romanesque Sculpture*, London, 1953.
André Grabar and Carl Nordenfalk, *Romanesque Painting*, Geneva, 1958.
Henri Focillon, *The Art of the West, Volume 1: Romanesque Art*, New York and London, 1963.

CHAPTER 6: GOTHIC ART

Peter Brieger, *English Art 1216-1307*, Oxford, 1957.
Richard Vaughan, *Matthew Paris* Cambridge, England, 1958.
Jean Porcher, *Medieval French Miniatures* New York, 1959.
Paul Frankl, *Gothic Architecture*, (Pelican History of Art) London, 1963.
John White, *Art and Architecture in Italy 1250-1400*, (Pelican History of Art) London, 1965.
George Henderson, *Gothic Art*, London, 1965.

CHAPTER 1

# IMPERIAL ROMAN ART

The continuity of the classical tradition has been, until the 20th century, one of the most striking aspects of Western art. It is to the Romans that we owe the survival of the Greek tradition through the centuries of the empire, and its transformation into the art of the Byzantine and early Christian world. Furthermore, the revival of the classical tradition at the time of the Renaissance took its inspiration not directly from the Greek world but from the Graeco-Roman tradition as it was rediscovered in Italy.

This brief introduction discusses some aspects of the Roman age which illustrate the continuity of the classical tradition and the emergence of new techniques and sources of inspiration in the later part of the period.

*One of the great features of Roman life was the "triumph" or procession of a victorious general on his return from a war. All his booty would be carried through the streets, much as in this late 15th-century painting by Mantegna* (A).

(A) ANDREA MANTEGNA Corselet Bearers, about 1486-94
*Hampton Court, London, Royal Collection*

## Greek influences in the 3rd and 2nd centuries B.C.

A frenzy of collecting and looting of sculpture, paintings, and other works of art marks the first phase of direct Roman contact with the artistic centers of the Greek world. Enormous booty was brought to Rome in the 3rd and 2nd centuries B.C. to adorn the triumphal processions of Roman generals, and this created an enthusiasm for Greek art that ensured the survival of Greek tradition into the Roman Empire. By the 2nd century B.C. the Romans had succeeded the Hellenistic kings as the chief patrons of Greek artists, and a wealthy Roman of the time of Cicero (106-43 B.C.) would have had the walls of his house painted in Greek style, its floors paved with Greek mosaics,

*Unfortunately most Greek original statuary has been lost or destroyed, but in Roman times its popularity was such that a large number of copies were made. Many of these have survived.*

*A generally accepted survival of a Greek original is the* Hermes *by Praxiteles* (A), *which was found in 1877 and of which no copies appear to have been made.*

*Three of the most copied statues were the* Diadoumenos *and the* Doryphoros, *both by Polycleitos, and the* Discobolos *by Myron* (B, C, D).

(A) PRAXITELES Hermes with the Infant Dionysos, about 350 B. C.
*Olympia, Greece, Museum*

(B) POLYCLEITOS Diadoumenos
about 440 B. C. (Roman copy)
*Athens, National Museum*

(D) MYRON Discobolos, 460-450 B. C. (Roman copy)
*Rome, Museo Nazionale Romano*

(C) POLYCLEITOS Doryphoros, about 450 B. C. (Roman copy)
*Naples, Museo Nazionale*

(A) Ceremony of the Census: from the Altar of Domitius Ahenobarbus, late 1st century B. C.
*Paris, Louvre*

and the niches filled with copied masterpieces of Greek sculpture. The Romans of the period also began to make demands upon Greek artists that could not be satisfied simply by imitation of an admired past. A Roman patrician or nobleman, when he commissioned a Greek to carve his portrait, would demand the kind of realism that suited his own traditions of portraiture. A successful general might commission a commemorative sculpture or painting which he wanted to be a factual record of events, like the ceremony of the census shown on the well-known relief from the so-called Altar of Domitius Ahenobarbus (A, B). He might get a Greek architect to design a commemorative building that was essentially Roman in form though it might be decorated in Greek style. In these combinations of Roman ideas and Greek artistic skill are to be found the beginnings of a specifically Roman art that is best explained by the idea of "Greek art in the service of Rome." The artists were mainly Greeks but the ideas and purpose were Roman.

(B) Altar of Domitius Ahenobarbus, late 1st century B.C.
*Paris, Louvre*

## The beginnings of official Roman art

Until the time of the first Roman emperor, Augustus (27 B.C.-14 A.D.), the patronage of Greek artists was almost entirely private. With the creation of the Roman Empire there began an official demand for sculpture and painting to commemorate public events and persons that had a purely Roman inspiration and direction. The great artistic achievements of the Roman age belong to this official art—to commemorative relief sculpture and to imperial portraiture. But at the same time there was an immense output of copies and adaptations of Greek sculpture and painting that continued to satisfy the private taste of the Romans of the Empire and has provided us with so much indirect knowledge of the lost masterpieces of the Greek world.

## Imperial art and the classical tradition

To summarize the development of art during the Roman period it may be said that the classical ideal, typified by what has survived of the sculpture and painting from the reign of Hadrian (117-138 A.D.), remained unchallenged until later in the 2nd century A.D. It was then that new trends, directly opposed to classical form and expressing new ideas, began to appear, and it is the understanding of these that makes an essential prelude to a knowledge of Byzantine and medieval art. The assessment of this development can best be discussed from the three aspects of Roman Imperial art that are the most characteristic contributions of the age. The first is commemorative relief sculpture decorating the great buildings of Rome; the second, portrait sculpture; and the third, painting. In the case of the last the evidence is drawn not from official painting, of which almost none has survived, but from the interior decoration of private houses and tombs.

## Commemorative relief sculpture

The first great official monument of the Roman Empire is the Altar of the Augustan Peace, the *Ara Pacis*, erected in Rome between 13 and 9 B.C. (C). Its sculptured decoration is a magnificent expression of the

(C) Altar of the Augustan Peace, 13-9 B.C.
*Rome*

A

B

(A) Floral scroll ornament: from the Altar of the Augustan Peace, 13-9 B. C.
*Rome*

(B) Processional frieze: from the Altar of the Augustan Peace, 13-9 B. C.
*Rome*

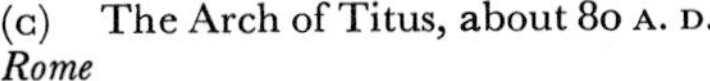

(C) The Arch of Titus, about 80 A. D.
*Rome*

(D) The Triumph of Titus: from the Arch of Titus, about 80 A. D.
*Rome*

C

D

ideals and hopes of a new era. The Tellus panel symbolizes by means of an allegory in Hellenistic style the peace and prosperity of the Roman world; the processional frieze (p. 22 B) is both a straightforward record of an event, and a grand and dignified conception inspired by classical Greek art. The exquisite floral ornament that decorates the building is carved by Greek craftsmen in the finest Hellenistc style (p. 22 A). The processional frieze stands at the beginning of a Roman tradition of historical relief. It makes a fairly successful attempt to achieve realism by using recessive planes of relief to show depth and space.

For another century or more, sculptors continued to concern themselves with these problems, and the most successful attempt at this three-dimensional relief sculpture is to be found in the famous processional panel from the passage-way of the Arch of Titus (p. 23), about 80 A.D., which gives the impression of real life and movement caught momentarily by the spectator. Not all Roman historical relief attempts this kind of "realism." Greek allegorical figures are often introduced into historical scenes, and the idea of imperial apotheosis brings gods and men into an easy relationship in the same scene.

(A) The Column of Trajan, early 2nd century A.D.
*Rome*

(B) The Column of Trajan (detail) early 2nd century A. D.
*Rome*

The reliefs on the Column of Trajan (about 110 A.D.) (A, B), illustrating the emperor's Dacian campaigns, adopt a factual style, based no doubt on eye-witness accounts. The reliefs that spiral round the shaft of the column are shown in what is called the continuous narrative method, in which the scenes merge into one another against a continuous background. The method has been thought to be a Roman development, strongly influenced by the contemporary methods of book illustration. The allegorical manner was preferred in the time of Hadrian and the Antonine emperors in the 2nd century, and the big panel compositions of this period are often pompous and unnatural in feeling (p. 26). An inevitable reaction to this style comes in the late 2nd and 3rd centuries as part of a change in artistic ideas that seems to derive from many different sources—a "popular" reaction in Rome itself and strong influences from the artistic traditions of the eastern Roman provinces.

Some of the characteristics of this change may be seen in the contrast between the reliefs on the column of Trajan and those of the column of Marcus Aurelius (about 180 A.D.) that followed the same design and much the same principle of decoration (p. 27). The artists of the later monument seemed to be more concerned with expressing the horror and suffering of war than with giving a factual record of events, and to do this they were prepared to distort the features, exaggerate gestures, and pay less attention to modeling and proportion. The term "expressionism" has been used to describe the tendencies opposed to the organic naturalism of Hellenistic art: a new taste that accepts crudities of composition, uncertainties of proportion, and careless

B

(A) The Apotheosis of Emperor Antoninus and his wife Faustina: from the base of the Column of Antoninus Pius, after 161 A. D.
*Rome, Vatican, Museum*

carving, and concentrates more on the expression of ideas and feelings. These tendencies can be studied in the rich series of 3rd-century A.D. sculptured sarcophagi. Some, like the "philosopher" sarcophagus of the Lateran Museum (p. 28 A), show the hopes and aspirations of those who lived in the troubled times of the late Roman Empire; others, like the Ludovisi battle sarcophagus (p. 29 B), imply the triumph of death over human suffering. This is the world into which Christianity was to come as the dominant force, and this is the art

(B) The Massacre of the Barbarians: from the Column of Marcus Aurelius, about 180 A. D.
*Rome*

in which it was to find its own inspiration. In the reliefs of the Arch of Constantine (about 313 A.D.), the tendencies in late Roman sculpture come completely to the fore. A rigid frontality has become the rule; the sculptor is no longer interested in problems of space and perspective, but has devised a symbolic rendering of a scene in a manner that could also serve the fundamental need for spiritual expression in Christian art and was to develop into a completely new artistic vision in the hieratic art of Byzantium (p. 29 C-F).

A

(A) The "Philosopher" Sarcophagus, possibly that of Emperor Gallienus, about 268 A. D.
*Rome, Lateran Museum*

(B) The Ludovisi Battle Sarcophagus
*Rome, Lateran Museum*

(C) The Arch of Constantine, about 313 A. D.
*Rome*

(D) The Lion Hunt: from the Arch of Constantine, about 313 A. D.
*Rome*

(E) The Boar Hunt: from the Arch of Constantine, about 313 A. D.
*Rome*

(F) Constantine Distributing Largess: from the Arch of Constantine, about 313 A. D.
*Rome*

C

B

D

E

F

(A) Head of Vespasian, about 70 A. D.
*London, British Museum*

## Portrait sculpture

The history of the art of portraiture in Imperial Rome also illustrates the same artistic development as the imperial relief sculpture. The stark realism of late Republican portraiture is in the last years of the last century B.C. transformed by the skill and delicacy of Hellenistic carving into a manner that, although firmly grounded in nature, nevertheless idealizes human features (p. 32). These characteristics are best visible in the idealized official portraits of the Emperor Augustus, of which the finest is the famous statue from the Villa of Livia at Prima Porta (D). It shows the emperor in military dress; the reliefs on his breastplate commemorate an event of which he was enormously proud—the return, in 20 B.C., of the standards captured by the Parthians at the Battle of Carrhae. The pose derives from a classical Greek statue, and the face and figure show the emperor as he wished to appear to the world. Like the historical reliefs, imperial portrait sculpture has its grand manner and its more intimate naturalistic style. There are portraits of Augustus that show a gentler, more sensitive man in civilian dress, though they are none the less idealized in conception.

The portraiture of a reign depends very largely on the taste of a particular emperor. Under the Flavian emperors there was a reaction

(B) Head of Hadrian, early 2nd century A. D.
*Rome, Museo Nazionale Romano*

(C) Bust of Marcus Aurelius, about 175 A. D.
*Rome, Museo Nazionale Romano*

(D) Statue of Emperor Augustus: from the Villa of Livia at Prima Porta, about 14 A. D.
*Rome, Vatican, Museum*

(A) Republican portrait: Statue of a Man Carrying Busts of his Ancestors, early 1st century A. D.
*Rome, Palazzo Barberini*

against the idealizing tradition in the down-to-earth portrait studies of Vespasian (69-79 A.D.) (p. 30 A) and his son Titus (79-81 A.D.) that seems to owe much to the Republican traditions of portraiture. Under Trajan and Hadrian, the idealizing trend comes to the fore again. It is most clearly seen in the bearded portraits of the Emperor Hadrian (p. 30 B) and the statues of his favourite Antinous (B), who died in 130 A.D., and whose portraits were to be found in many parts of the Roman world. In the portraits of Marcus Aurelius (161-180 A.D.) (p. 30 C), there is a fundamental change toward the same kind of "expressionism" that is found in the historical reliefs of the period. The sculptors seemed to be attempting much more than an interpretation of the physical characteristics of a man. They tried to bring out elements of character and experience, and to do so they simplified and even distorted the features and expressions. In many of the portraits of the 3rd century, such as the head of the Emperor Trajan Decius (C), are to be seen, as was probably intended, the sufferings and tragedies of the times through the eyes of a man. At first glance, the hard dry style of the portraits of the time of Diocletian, at the end of the 3rd century, is reminiscent of Republican portraiture; but the sculpture, by simplifying the form, is trying to convey a completely different vision that led only a few years later to a new conception of portraiture in which nature was transformed into the inhuman detachment of a purely symbolic rendering of the majesty of the emperor (D).

(B) Statue of Antinous (detail) about 130 A.D.
*Delphi, Greece, Museum*

(C) Head of Emperor Trajan Decius, about 250 A.D.
*Rome, Capitoline Museum*

(D) Head of Constantine: from the Basilica of Constantine, about 313 A.D.
*Rome, Palazzo dei Conservatori*

## Roman decorative painting

Our knowledge of Roman painting derives not from official Roman art but from the decoration of private houses and tombs. From the 2nd century B.C. to 79 A.D., the history of Roman decorative painting is well documented by the walls of houses at Pompeii and Herculaneum, together with some fine examples from Rome and elsewhere in Italy. After 79 A.D., the evidence is much more fragmentary—a few houses, painted tombs, and, from the 3rd century onwards, the paintings of Christian catacombs in Rome.

The earliest of the Roman styles of interior decoration is common to a very large area of the Hellenistic world and was certainly introduced into Italy from the Greek east. In this style the wall is made to look as though it were faced with marble slabs in different colors, imitating the masonry construction of a Hellenistic Greek building (p. 167). This earliest style established the architectural basis of all subsequent Roman interior decoration. The so-called second Pompeian style transformed this basic scheme by producing an apparent recession of the wall with the aid of perspective vistas of architecture, derived, it seems, from Hellenistic theater design, by opening up a view into a park or garden, or by showing figure scenes and landscape behind columns. The big frieze paintings, like those from the Villa of the Mysteries at Pompeii (p. 168), or the Odyssey landscapes now in the Vatican (p. 169), are associated with this second style of decoration. Later fashions in decorative design were to treat the wall, or part of it, as a blank screen apparently concealing vistas, or sometimes as a flat surface divided into panels by patterns of fantastic architecture, like the "grotesques" of Nero's Golden House (p. 170) that inspired Raphael's work in the Loggie of the Vatican (A, B). The "closed" styles of wall decoration often incorporated panel pictures in painted frames. A later style of about 70 A.D. again introduced baroque visions of architecture in the background.

(A) RAPHAEL Detail from Loggia decoration, 1519
*Rome, Vatican*

(B) RAPHAEL The Story of Jesus: from Loggia ceiling, 1519
*Rome, Vatican*

(c) The Trojan Horse: from Pompeii, 1st cent. A.D.
*Naples, Museo Nazionale*

(d) The Trojan Horse (detail): from Pompeii, 1st century A. D.
*Naples, Museo Nazionale*

In the schemes of decoration the artists incorporated a rich variety of motifs—figured friezes and panels, landscapes, landscapes with figures, still-lifes, portraits, and so on. The sources of these pictures are for the most part Greek, though it is not always easy to assess how far the Roman versions differ from their originals and what are the distinctively Roman elements in the pictures. The problem is clearly seen in the ambitious frieze compositions of the second-style walls—for example, the frieze showing the ceremonies of initiation into Dionysiac rites on the walls of a room in the Villa of the Mysteries at Pompeii, where the figures are clearly inspired by Hellenistic art though the whole composition is probably the work of a Roman of the period (p. 171). The same problem arises in the case of the landscape scenes illustrating the tenth and eleventh books of the Odyssey, which were found in a house on the Esquiline Hill, Rome, and are now in the Vatican Library (p. 169). An increasing interest in landscape is certainly a characteristic of late Hellenistic painting, but it is not known how much these panoramic scenes, shown in depth from a high viewpoint with considerable use of linear and aerial perspective, owe to the style of the period in which they were painted. As in the case of sculpture, painters of the Roman age were greatly interested in the problems of space and perspective. They never, in fact, achieved either a consistent linear or aerial perspective, but they went a long way toward the creation of masterly illusionistic effects such as those in the haunting picture of the introduction of the Trojan Horse into the city of Troy (c, d) and in several landscapes of the period (p. 172). These pictures are painted in what may be called an impressionistic style with the figures modeled in patches of color and light and shade.

(A) DIOSCURIDES OF SAMOS Mendicant and Musicians, about 100 B. C.
*Naples, Museo Nazionale*

(B) Detail from mosaic floor, 4th century A. D.
*Piazza Armerina, Sicily, Villa Romana del Casale*

Although they were the work of modest artisans, the big panel pictures associated with compositions of the third and fourth Pompeian styles have a special interest for the light they throw on lost masterpieces of Greek painting. There is no doubt that many of them were copied from famous Greek pictures of the classical and Hellenistic periods, and several replicas of some of them survive. A typical example is the picture showing the hero Perseus freeing Andromeda (p. 173). Our knowledge of later Greek painting derives from these Roman copies though the evidence must be used with caution since the replicas differ very considerably from one another. But not all the subject matter of Roman decorative painting is Greek. The taste for garden vistas, like the superb garden room from the Villa of Livia at Prima Porta (p. 174), seems to be Roman, as is the love of still-life and *trompe l'oeil* compositions (p. 175).

After the destruction of Pompeii in 79 A.D., information about the development of Roman painting is very fragmentary. The basic schemes of decoration remained the same, and the surviving painted walls from Ostia and elsewhere are mostly inferior or simplified versions of schemes already known at Pompeii. From the style of the figure paintings only the broadest conclusions can be drawn. Under Trajan and Hadrian in the first part of the 2nd century there was a revival of classicism with its clear-cut outline and precise modeling in color, and this seems to have been followed in the Antonine period (138-192 A.D.) by a revival of the impressionistic manner.

*A panel picture is a distinct portion of a wall or ceiling painting contained in a painted frame or border. (This should not be confused with the use of the term denoting a moveable picture usually painted on wood.) Such wall paintings, however, are often transferred on to wooden panels for the sake of preservation in museums. Wall mosaics contained within a clearly defined area are also referred to as panels.*

**Mosaic decoration**

The tradition of mosaic decoration in Imperial Rome is closely related to that of painting. The earliest mosaics from Pompeii are executed in minute tesserae (small cubes of colored stone) and are imitations of Greek paintings like the famous Alexander mosaic from the House of the Faun at Pompeii (p. 176), believed to be copied from a 4th-century B.C. painting. *Trompe l'oeil* pictures, landscape scenes, and scenes of Egyptian inspiration seem to go back to Hellenistic sources (A). In the 2nd and 3rd centuries A.D., carpet patterns, based upon geometric designs and incorporating figures and other pictorial details, are the most typical form of mosaic decoration, but big over-all figure compositions are also found and come into their own in the late Roman period. Among the finest examples are the famous 4th-century mosaics from Piazza Armerina in Sicily (B). In the 4th century some of the finest wall and ceiling decoration was carried out in mosaic, setting a fashion that was to become a characteristic feature of early Christian and Byzantine art. One of the finest surviving examples is the vault decoration dating from the mid-4th century from the ambulatory of the church of Santa Costanza in Rome (p. 177).

CHAPTER 2

# EARLY CHRISTIAN ART

A

## The decline of the Roman Empire

As the Roman Empire slowly declined over a long period from the 3rd to the 5th century A.D., so did the impetus that had been given to official art by a strong Roman state and an expanding economy. The masses turned to the mystery religions of the east for spiritual comfort in an age of turmoil at home, and there was widespread interest in Judaism until it was outshone by Christianity.

Since the very existence of the empire was threatened by barbarian invaders, loyalty became a spiritual issue and the imperial choice of a religious cult was an expression of imperial destiny. At this time the Christian church gathered momentum—Origen (about 185-253) had made Christianity intellectually respectable—and it could no longer be ignored. Persecution by Decius, Valerian, and Diocletian had failed; and when Galerius, the then ruler of the Eastern Roman Empire, invaded Italy, he turned to the Christians whose god, he felt, had afflicted him. It was thus he who, having previously persuaded Diocletian to persecute the Christians, now issued an Edict of Toleration. But this act did not ensure him victory, and it was Constantine, after his own victory at the Milvian Bridge near Rome, who in 313 proclaimed, with Licinius, the Edict of Milan whereby Christianity became a tolerated religion.

## The rise of Christianity

The earliest examples of Christian art belong among the artistic developments that took place in the last centuries of the Roman Empire. Since the early Christians lived in a highly cultured age, it was perfectly logical that they should have taken advantage of current trends in the figurative arts and used them to express their own religious and spiritual aspirations. Although they adopted, for lack of an alternative, the common current artistic language, they nevertheless expressed the ideals of the gospel in a distinctive style of their own.

It is significant, too, that the artistic testimony of the early Christians, who pinned their faith to a better life to come, was revealed in the

(A) Early Christian sign: anchor and fish, 3rd century A. D.
*Rome, Priscilla Catacomb*

(B) Roman catacomb: burial place of early Christian martyrs
*Artist's impression*

(C) Heavenly Jerusalem, 230-240 A. D.
*Rome, Hypogeum of the Aurelii*

(D) Adam and Eve, mid-6th century
*Rome, S. Pietro and S. Marcellino Catacomb*

pictorial and sculptural decoration of tombs—a clear indication that their chief interest was not centered on life in this world but in the next, beyond the limits of time.

## Painting

The earliest Christian paintings are probably those in the catacombs in Rome (B). These paintings are often found decorating the walls of crypts or subterranean caves where martyrs' relics were buried and venerated, as well as on the vaults and walls of the recesses, usually square, intended for several tombs belonging perhaps to one family. They are less frequent in the corridors to the tombs. The technique most commonly used was that of fresco painting.

Not all these early Christian paintings reached a high artistic standard. They failed to achieve a lyrical expression or true poetic feeling, because they were painted mostly by simple tradesmen and artisans who repeated certain set themes derived from a popular art distinct from the traditions of the upper class. They worked with varying degrees of skill, but with little regard for aesthetics. The decline of classical form in late Roman art must be partly explained by this revival of a popular element. In the scene of the Heavenly Jerusalem in the hypogeum (burial chamber) of the Aurelii in Rome (C) the bird's eye view has been attributed to a popular source. The supreme indifference to classical form in the figures of Adam and Eve (D) from the catacomb of San Pietro and San Marcellino in Rome may have the same origin.

B

C

D

(A, B) Wall decorations in the Ampliatus crypt, about 150 A. D.
*Rome, Domitilla Catacomb*

(C) The Samaritan Woman at the Well, late 2nd century A. D.
*Rome, Praetextatus Catacomb*

## Chronology of catacomb paintings: 2nd-3rd century

The chronology of the catacomb paintings remains controversial, especially the date of the earliest ones. In the 19th century they were thought to date back to the 1st century, but today they are believed to start in the 2nd century.

Possibly the oldest Roman tomb paintings are those decorating the Ampliatus crypt in the Domitilla catacomb on the Via Ardeatina (A, B). At the foot of the wall is a painted dado of imitation marble inlay, and above that a screen looking like a series of pier-glasses formed by a succession of slender colonnettes that nevertheless give the impression of performing a real structural function. This decorative scheme definitely stems from the so-called Pompeian fourth style, and appears to represent a room in a private house. Comparison with a fresco at Ostia has led to a dating of approximately the mid-2nd century.

The frescoes adorning the vaults and some of the large niches in the Flavii hypogeum, also in the Domitilla catacomb, are dated a few years later. Various geometrical patterns of rectangles, triangles, circles, and trapezoids stand out against a light background. The internal borders are made gay and attractive by various cheerful little flowers, bushes, birds, or other small creatures, sketched in with truly amazing freedom. This impressionistic technique is particularly noticeable in the famous little winged cupid who sits at the apex of one of these vaults and is remarkable for his graceful posture and the barely suggested flutter of his tiny wings (p. 178).

The vault of the main corridor to the hypogeum is particularly beautifully decorated. Along its length are two slender vine tendrils that twist and twine with an unusual sense of lightness; the vines themselves, aided by the pale tones of the ceiling, seem to be bathed in a radiant light.

The paintings in the Urania cubicle in the Praetextatus catacomb, Rome, now established as the end of the 2nd century, contain scenes from the New Testament: the raising of Lazarus, the Samaritan woman at the well (C), and the much discussed Crowning with Thorns (D). The forms are rendered in terms of shading, but high-lighted with streaks of white and yellow applied at strategic points.

In the Lucina catacomb, Rome, there are paintings showing the symbolic fish, baskets of bread, and wine representing Christ and the Holy Eucharist. In the Callixtus catacomb, also in Rome, scenes reputed to be part of the Jonah cycle are painted on the vaults of the so-called Chambers of the Sacraments. These frescoes are probably early 3rd century, as are the frescoes in the Cappella Greca of the Priscilla catacomb, Rome. The earliest of these (the breaking of bread is one example) stand out clearly against a reddish background (p.

179); the others, painted shortly afterwards, the cycle of Susanna for example, have a contrasting light-yellowish background (E).

Another painting executed in the first half of the 3rd century is the famous *Arenarium Madonna and Child* in the adjoining section of the same catacomb (p. 180). This, the earliest known picture of the Virgin, seems to radiate a powerful sense of humanity and realism.

Other frescoes of great artistic merit are those decorating the Aurelii hypogeum. Flanking various narrative scenes are the solemn figures of the Apostles, portrayed according to classical rhythms and proportions and with an extremely soft modeling of form. Scholars are almost unanimously agreed that these paintings should be dated somewhere between 225 and 240.

Approximately the same date has been assigned to the fresco depicting the sacrifice of Abraham in the Velata cubicle of the Priscilla catacomb, where the figure of the patriarch is contrasted against a light, clear background in an extremely well-balanced composition. It depicts the moment just before the sacrifice, when he stands beside his little son Isaac who is carrying a bundle of faggots on his back. A technique of short rapid brush-strokes has been used to pick out the flashes of white on eyes, nose, and chin of both figures (F).

The frescoes in the *domus ecclesiae* (house-church) and the synagogue at Dura Europos in Mesopotamia belong to the same period or even earlier. Dura Europos was a Roman frontier town, and was excavated in 1931. It had been captured and destroyed by the Persians in 256, so the finds there were of the greatest possible significance in helping to date these early frescoes. Those in the *domus ecclesiae*—showing scenes

(D) The Crowning with Thorns, late 2nd century A. D.
*Rome, Praetextatus Catacomb*

(E) Scene from the Cycle of Susanna, late 2nd century A. D.
*Rome, Priscilla Catacomb*

(F) The Sacrifice of Abraham, 225-240 A. D.
*Rome, Priscilla Catacomb*

from the Old and New Testaments—constitute the oldest baptistery frescoes in existence, while those in the synagogue provide the sole Hebrew example of walls covered entirely with paintings (p. 181). One of the most important features about the paintings at Dura Europos is their quantity and the immense range of subjects from both Testaments.

In Rome, the impressionistic technique proper appeared for the first time about the middle of the 3rd century. It had been somewhat restricted previously, but at this period it seems to have broken out in decisive fashion. It is typified by the heads of figures personifying the four seasons in a cubicle of the San Pietro and San Marcellino catacomb; they are depicted quite simply by patches of light and shadow but are nevertheless extraordinarily spirited (A, B, C, D).

One example of a plastic-structural style of painting, so-called because all the objects appear to stand out in sharp relief, is a group of praying figures, known as *orants*, in the Garden of Paradise in the Five Saints crypt of the Callixtus catacomb (p. 182).

(A, B, C, D) Figures personifying the Four Seasons, mid-3rd century A. D.
*Rome, S. Pietro and S. Marcellino Catacomb*

### 4th century

At the beginning of the 4th century there are further examples of the popular style of painting in which spontaneous narrative captures a feeling of *joie de vivre*. Typical examples are the realistic scene of a group of wine carriers in the wine casks chamber in the Priscilla catacomb (E), and the scene showing laborers building a house and working in the fields in the Trevius Justus hypogeum.

The great praying figures in the Coemeterium Maius of the Trasone catacomb appear to have been painted a little before the mid-4th century. In these figures there is a definite attempt to accentuate form by means of clear-cut outline, a pronounced sense of frontality, and a marked tendency to leave all facial expression to a few lines judiciously sketched in, especially the eyebrows, nose, and mouth. The eyes, generally large and outlined in black, seem to reflect a profound spiritual concentration (F, and p. 183).

About the middle of the 4th century there appeared a new classical manner (also called the *stile bello*). The most important examples are the numerous paintings discovered in Rome in 1955, in a hypogeum on the Via Latina. Side by side with scenes of pagan myths are others that are typically Christian or drawn from incidents of daily life; one of the scenes appears to be an anatomy lesson (G, H).

The same classical elements persisted throughout the second half of the 4th century. The figures continue to be characterized by a solid, clearly defined structural form, although occasionally there is a sudden splash of color with the relative interplay of light and shadow. Among representative paintings are some magnificent frescoes, in

(E) Wine Carriers, early 4th century A. D.
*Rome, Priscilla Catacomb*

(F) The Virgin and Child, mid-4th century A. D.
*Rome, Trasone Catacomb*

(G) The Samaritan Woman at the Well, mid-4th century A. D.
*Rome, Via Latina*

(H) The Anatomy Lesson, mid-4th century A. D.
*Rome, Via Latina*

which the figures have been elongated, in the crypt of the Church of San Giovanni and San Paolo in Rome.

Toward the end of the 4th and at the beginning of the 5th century there seems to be an echo of basilical decoration in some of the catacomb frescoes. For example, the figure of Christ among his Apostles decorating one of the niches in the crypt of the Domitilla catacomb has much in common with the apsidal mosaic in the Church of Santa Pudenziana, especially in the way the Redeemer has been isolated from the two groups of disciples (A, and p. 184).

The fresco in the catacomb of San Pietro and San Marcellino is divided into two superimposed registers: Christ enthroned between St. Peter and St. Paul in one, and the Mystic Lamb between the four saints venerated in that particular catacomb in the other (B). This fresco also dates back to the end of the 4th or the early 5th century. Apart from the Saviour, all the figures are tall and slender; they seem to lack solidity, to be stiff and stylized, indicative of a new conception of art and a break from previous tradition.

Generally speaking, fresco backgrounds are by this time no longer landscapes; they have mostly become abstract. The figures have assumed a stiff, frontal pose. This tendency, seen in some 5th century frescoes in the catacombs of San Gennaro dei Poveri and San Gaudioso in Naples, was also evident in Rome, where Byzantine influences were beginning to appear. This is particularly evident in the famous fresco of the Virgin enthroned between the martyrs Felix and Adauctus in the Commodilla catacomb (C).

(A) Christ among His Apostles, late 4th/early 5th century A. D.
*Rome, Domitilla Catacomb*

(B) Christ Enthroned between St. Peter and St. Paul; and the Mystic Lamb, late 4th/early 5th century A. D.
*Rome, S. Pietro and S. Marcellino Catacomb*

(C) The Virgin Enthroned between St. Felix and St. Adauctus, first half of the 6th century
*Rome, Commodilla Catacomb*

## Mosaics

The most outstanding feature of early Christian mosaics is that they are very closely allied to architecture; they and the structure they decorate are an indivisible aesthetic whole.

Mosaic was a favorite form of early Christian art: it was like a heavily jewel-encrusted and many-colored cloak that enveloped apses, triumphal arches, and cupolas, and the vaults of baptisteries, basilicas, and mausoleums.

### 3rd-4th century

The oldest extant Christian mosaics are those decorating the mausoleum of the Julii, a small building in the catacomb under St. Peter's excavated between 1940 and 1949. The decoration covers a large section of the vault on which the chariot of the sun stands out in brilliant splendor against the twisting stems of a spreading vine-trellis. This mosaic, with its typically Hellenistic grace and liveliness, may well date back to the end of the 3rd century.

The same artistic trend must have featured in the mosaics (now almost all lost, though the drawings for them are still extant) of the cupola in the mausoleum of Constantina at Rome, dated the second quarter of the 4th century. Those which do exist, in the annular vault, show the busts of two figures amidst gracefully trailing vine-stems and light-hearted scenes of small children making merry over the grape harvest (D, and p. 177).

(D) Detail of ceiling mosaic, mid-4th century A.D.
*Rome, S. Costanza*

(A) St. Peter Receiving the Law, 4th century A. D.
*Rome, S. Costanza*

(B) Christ Giving the Keys to St. Peter, 4th century A. D.
*Rome, S. Costanza*

However, the apsidal mosaics of *St. Peter Receiving the Law* and *Christ Giving the Keys to St. Peter* are evidence of an altogether different trend, which brings them very much in line with the artistic precepts underlying the frescoes in the Roman catacombs (A, B). Another funeral monument whose mosaics are similar in style and subject—they also depict scenes taken from the Old and New Testaments—is the mausoleum of Centcelles near Tarragona in Spain. These mosaics are perhaps as early as mid-4th century.

**5th century**

The mosaics in the baptistery of the Church of San Giovanni in Fonte, adjoining the Church of San Gennaro, in Naples may date back to the end of the 4th century or the beginning of the 5th (D). The cupola in this particular baptistery has a crown at the top containing the *Chrismon* (the sacred monogram) set in a starry sky, and is divided radially into sections. These contain various scenes from the New Testament and, lower down, the symbols of the Evangelists and various figures of saints. Part of this decoration, where the figures are portrayed in a more plastic, modeled fashion, and in brighter colors, was executed by mosaic workers trained both in Roman and local tradition. Another part, where the figures are less clearly defined, flatter-looking, and paler-toned, was executed by mosaic workers who were more susceptible to the spell-binding influence of Oriental art.

There is an interesting diversity of style in the contemporary mosaics in the Santa Matrona chapel in the Church of San Prisco, near Santa Maria Capua Vetere. Here the four curved segments of the cross vault, decorated with trailing vine-stems on a dark blue background, seem to be a clear indication of Hellenistic-Oriental influence (C). In this way they differ from the symbols of the Evangelists, whose bold treatment is rooted in classical Roman art.

During the early part of the 5th century there was one great mosaic impregnated with an awe-inspiring, monumental atmosphere. It decorates the semi-dome in the apse of the Church of Santa Pudenziana and shows Christ enthroned amidst His Apostles, gathered together in front of a curved portico (p. 184). This is an outstanding work executed in a well-balanced range of colors. Although inspired by the new religious ideas, it is the last mosaic masterpiece in Rome which could be labeled classical art.

The same period probably saw the execution of the mosaics in the octagonal chapel of Sant'Aquilino in the Church of San Lorenzo Maggiore at Milan. Themes found in the catacomb frescoes are repeated in the apse; for instance, there is one pastoral scene (it

(C) Cross vault mosaic, 5th century A. D.
*S. Prisco, near Santa Maria Capua Vetere, Santa Matrona Chapel*

(D) Detail of mosaic in cupola pendentive, late 4th/early 5th century A. D.
*Naples, S. Giovanni in Fonte, Baptistery*

(A) Christ among His Apostles, 5th century A. D.
*Milan, S. Lorenzo Maggiore, S. Aquilino Chapel*

(B) The Christian Church of the Jews, 5th century A. D.
*Rome, S. Sabina*

could be Elijah being swept up to heaven) that has a graceful Hellenistic air about it, and another of Christ among his Apostles who are ranged on two different registers, something hitherto unknown. Moreover, instead of being white, the background to this composition is, for the first time, very largely gold (A).

The classicist tradition, like that at Santa Pudenziana, is still evident in the internal façade of the Church of Santa Sabina in Rome, erected during Pope Sixtus III's reign (432-440). Here *The Christian Church of the Jews* and *The Christian Church of the Gentiles* are shown on either side of a large inscription. However, the colors are quieter and not broken up into small patches; the modeling of the human figures shows less skilled draftsmanship, in spite of the fact that the robes follow the body movement closely in the way they fall (B).

The mosaics decorating one of the two apses opposite each other in the entrance to the Lateran Baptistery were executed in the same period, but they are interesting mainly from the decorative point of view. The apse is entirely filled with an extremely harmonious pattern of large green acanthus scrolls picked out in gold highlights on an indigo ground (C). The mosaics on the triumphal arch and the central nave in the Church of Santa Maria Maggiore in Rome also belong to this period. They show the iconographical cycle of the

(c) Apse mosaic, 432-440 A. D.
*Rome, Lateran Baptistery*

(d) The Annunciation; and the Doubt of St. Joseph, 432-440 A. D.
*Rome, S. Maria Maggiore*

*Childhood of Christ*, where the individual episodes are frequently inspired by apocryphal texts (d). The figures in these Oriental-style mosaics are made to stand out not so much by their contours as by their bright and enamel-like colors, which are sometimes graduated and sometimes broken up by startling contrasts. The artist often used a static arrangement of figures and symmetrical groups in order to produce scenes with a calm, slow rhythm and a solemn atmosphere.

On the other hand, there is a much stronger Hellenistic influence in the mosaics along the central nave, which contain 27 scenes (originally

(A) Abraham and the Three Angels, 432-440 A. D.
*Rome, S. Maria Maggiore*

(B) The Story of Jacob, 432-440 A. D.
*Rome, S. Maria Maggiore*

42) showing episodes in the life of Abraham, Jacob, Moses, and Joshua (A, B). Occasionally the scenes take the form of two superimposed panels, which has led to the belief that illustrated manuscripts inspired them. The panels were not all executed by the same craftsmen; they clearly belonged to different groups, as can be seen from the manner of modeling the figures, which at times are rendered in a bold plastic *chiaroscuro* and at times appear much flatter. The individual scenes in the mosaics on the triumphal arch have infinitely more variety and freedom of composition; they have brighter colors and a more episodic quality, while from a pictorial point of view there is a stronger effort to create a three-dimensional effect, to make the faces of the figures expressive, and occasionally to take advantage of some really bold color combinations.

There is a fresh Hellenistic air that brings new life to parts of the mosaics in the mausoleum of Galla Placidia in Ravenna, which has been dated, probably quite correctly, to the second half of the 5th century (C, and p. 185). What is unusual about these mosaics is the naturalism in the figure of the Good Shepherd, rendered in softly flowing lines in the middle of a delightful pastoral setting with a

(C) The Good Shepherd, 5th century A. D.
*Ravenna, Mausoleum of Galla Placidia*

blue background. The rest of the decorative scheme reveals interesting discrepancies in style, since the barrel vaults and the cupola are essentially decorative, while the lunettes with the eight Apostles show a certain rigidity and schematization.

There is a lively decoration with sharply contrasting colors in the cupola of the Baptistery of the Orthodox at Ravenna, commissioned by Bishop Neon shortly after the middle of the 5th century. The central medallion, with the baptism of Christ on a gold background, is surrounded by two great concentric bands. On the first, the twelve Apostles—divided into two groups and contrasted against an indigo ground—form a regular procession carrying their symbolic crowns; their faces are rendered to some extent realistically. On the second band is a series of porticoes and colonnades with thrones and altars, intended to express the concept of the *etimasia* (readiness) in abstract terms (D, and p. 186).

The mosaics in the cupola of the Baptistery of the Arians in Ravenna may have been created in the late 5th or early 6th century (p. 187). All the figures, those on the central medallion showing the baptism of Christ and those depicting the procession of the Apostles, show up boldly against an unrealistic gold background.

Only a few vestiges of decoration in the old Baptistery of Albenga remain today, and these are to be found in the apse opposite the entrance, where the *Chi Rho* (the monogrammatic cross ☧), flanked by the Alpha and Omega, is enclosed by three repeating concentric circles (possibly an allusion to the Holy Trinity) that range from pale to deep blue. The outermost circle is surrounded by twelve doves, symbolizing the twelve Apostles. The date of this mosaic may be put in the second half of the 5th century.

In Casaranello in Terra d'Otranto there is also a small cruciform oratory that is architecturally similar to the mausoleum of Galla Placidia. In one of the barrel vaults there are still some decorative motifs, and in the cupola is a starry sky (at the center of which is a cross in yellow tesserae) divided into two concentric scenes, one lighter at the top and the other darker at the outer edge. This appears to correspond with the Oriental idea of the sky. It may therefore have been the work of Oriental artists, especially as at the end of the 5th century, a possible date for the oratory, the Emperor Zeno is known to have sent some workers in mosaic from Constantinople to the Bishop of Siponto to decorate the Church of San Giovanni Battista there.

The mosaics in the Chapel of San Vittore in Ciel d'Oro, adjoining San Ambrogio, Milan, may date back to the end of the 5th century. There is a flattened modeling and a transcendental quality in the faces of these Milanese saints, shown against intense blue walls, and in the face of St. Victor himself who stands out boldly against the gold of the cupola (E).

(D) The Baptism of Christ and the Twelve Apostles, 450-475 A. D.
*Ravenna, Baptistery of the Orthodox*

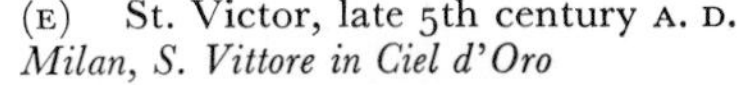

(E) St. Victor, late 5th century A. D.
*Milan, S. Vittore in Ciel d'Oro*

## 5th-6th century

The Archbishop's Palace at Ravenna, raised by Bishop Peter II (493-519), may be ascribed to the last few years of the 5th or the early 6th century. The vault of the oratory, supported by four arches decorated with medallions of the Apostles and saints, who stare with an intense, hypnotic gaze, provides a golden background for the four symbols of the Evangelists and for the four angels who are holding up a circular medallion enclosing the monogram of Christ (A, and p. 188). This might have been executed by mosaic workers from Ravenna who were influenced both by Hellenistic-Roman and Oriental art, as in the church, now called San Apollinare Nuovo, raised by Theodoric in

(A) Vault of the oratory, late 5th/early 6th century
*Ravenna, Archbishop's Palace*

(B) The Procession of Saints, about 560
*Ravenna, S. Apollinare Nuovo*

the third decade of the 6th century (C). In this basilica, the walls of the central nave are faced entirely with mosaics. The upper section shows, on the left, scenes of Christ's parables and the miracles he wrought, and on the right, scenes of the Redeemer's passion and some of the events after his death. The miracle scenes show a remarkably balanced composition and serenity of expression, while the Passion scenes show great vigor and intense emotion; such stylistic discrepancies in these two mosaic series would indicate that there were two different groups of artists at work.

However, the two magnificent processions of saints and martyrs which face each other on the bands below, are dated a little after 560 (B, and p. 189). These mosaics were executed when the church was made officially Catholic. There is infinite variety of vertical rhythm in the long procession, despite the limited movement, reminiscent of Oriental schematic works.

(C) S. Apollinare Nuovo, about 530
*Ravenna*

(A) S. Vitale, mid-6th century
*Ravenna*

The mosaics in the Church of St. Cosmas and St. Damian at Rome date from the reign of Pope Felix (III) IV (526-530). The semi-dome vault in the apse is decorated with an appearance of God in visible form. Christ is depicted on a wide stairway of clouds; below Him on either side are the saints Peter and Paul, Cosmas and Damian, together with Pope Felix (restored) and St. Theodore. The figure of the Redeemer seems particularly solemn and hieratic; it is quietly and undramatically drawn but full of light. However, the supernatural apparition has been interpreted in a naturalistic manner, so that the surrounding space is shown in clear perspective; the human figures are very solid and their features are sharp (p. 190).

The mosaics in the Church of San Vitale at Ravenna (A) are dated just before the middle of the 6th century. Those on the walls and presbytery vault are the work of artists trained in the Hellenistic-Roman tradition and are outstanding for their fluid narrative composition and

(B) Mosaics in the presbytery, mid-6th century
*Ravenna, S. Vitale*

(c) Center nave, mid-6th century
*Ravenna, S. Apollinare in Classe*

their pronounced naturalism and liveliness. Behind the figures, seen in a variety of poses, there is a highly atmospheric landscape (B).

The apsidal mosaics, executed by artists trained in the Byzantine tradition, are characterized by stiff frontal figures against a gold background. Christ is poised on the terrestrial globe between two archangels, St. Vitale, Bishop Ecclesius, and the two famous groups of Justinian's and Theodora's imperial processions (p. 191).

In the year after San Vitale was consecrated, 549, the Basilica of San Apollinare in Classe was dedicated (D). Here the semi-dome in the apse contains, in the upper section, a mosaic representing the *Transfiguration of Christ*, and, in the lower one, the solemn hieratic figure of St. Apollinare, the first Bishop of Ravenna, set against a lush green landscape (c, and p. 192).

The artist has here succeeded in blending naturalism and stylization, realistic figures and abstract forms. He has in fact given us a work of great inspiration and high artistic merit.

(D) S. Apollinare in Classe, mid-6th century
*Ravenna*

(A) Ram sarcophagus, possibly early 3rd century A. D.
*Rome, Lateran Mus.*

(B) Sarcophagus discovered at La Gayolle, France, early 3rd century A. D.
*Brignoles, France, Church of the Sacred Heart*

(C) Strigated sarcophagus, 3rd century A. D.
*Rome, S. Saba*

## Sculpture

The earliest examples of Christian sculpture are found, as are those of painting, within the framework of sepulchral art. Early Christian sculpture—or at least all that has survived—consists chiefly of marble sarcophagi.

Not all archaeologists are agreed on the date when the first Christian sarcophagi were carved. Many scholars thought it was about the middle of the 2nd century, but recently it has been thought that no Christian sculpture was produced before the middle of the 3rd century.

However, it is possible that the earliest known Christian sarcophagus is No. 181 in the Lateran Museum, Rome, discovered in the last century in a vineyard near the Via Salaria in Rome. This tomb has also been called the Ram Sarcophagus because of the two carved rams that decorate the fore-corners. Here the Good Shepherd and a female praying figure form the center of a group. Some of these figures are taking part in a scene that, although perhaps not catechistic, does not at any rate represent an event in the intellectual life of the deceased (A).

The stylistic parallels with reliefs of the time of the Emperor Severus encourage the belief that this piece of sculpture was carved in the last few years of the 2nd century, or possibly the beginning of the 3rd century. In other words, it was carved at a period of artistic evolution when artists were acutely conscious of the space surrounding their figures. Such figures were correctly weighted, each limb well balanced and proportioned; there is a feeling for the third dimension combined with a few pictorial details.

Another sarcophagus which stems from the same parentage as the Ram, but carved about 20 years later, is the one discovered at La Gayolle and now in the Church of the Sacred Heart at Brignoles in Provence. Its figures are spaced out and seem to exist independently of each other; there appears to be nothing to link them in any way. This is not therefore a fluid composition; on the contrary, it appears altogether static (B).

Contemporary with this type of sarcophagus, whose long façade is filled with evenly spaced figures, was another type adopted by the Christians and derived from pagan forms: the strigated sarcophagus, whose sides are enriched with rows of sinuous S-shaped fluting (C). This type was immensely popular during the 3rd century; as a rule the strigated areas may be found on either side of a central carved panel, while two more panels, also decorated with carved figures, are placed at either end of the façade. There are many scenes of people reading from scrolls, praying figures, the Good Shepherd, the Philosopher, or the Fisher of Men. Portraits of the deceased—just the bust framed by a circular medallion or shells—are frequent too.

(D) The Good Shepherd, mid-3rd century A. D. *Rome, Lateran Mus.*

(A) The Good Shepherd, mid-3rd century A. D.
*Rome, Capitoline Mus.*

About the middle of the 3rd century, the typical sarcophagus was strigated, with the figure of the Good Shepherd in the central panel and lions' heads at the angles.

The two small statues of the Good Shepherd in the Lateran Museum (p. 57 D) and the Capitoline Museum, Rome (A), are only a few years later. They show an extremely soft modeling, so delicate in fact that the planes blend smoothly into one another, almost as if they had lost all definition. Here is an echo of the classical trend which was established during the reign of the Emperor Gallienus (260-268 A.D.).

In the second half of the 3rd century the typical sarcophagus façade was filled with pastoral or rural scenes. In the center was a praying figure, while at the sides were figures of shepherds watching over their flocks.

Toward the end of the 3rd and at the beginning of the 4th century there emerged a new kind of sarcophagus, one whose façade is in the form of a continuous frieze where all the available space is filled by an unbroken chain of scenes, mostly drawn from episodes in the Old and New Testaments. The figures show a decided emphasis on the vertical. The carver wanted to introduce as many different Biblical scenes as he could, and crammed his figures closely together, giving a very real sense of overcrowding

This kind of sarcophagus was most common in the Constantinian period, and in the second quarter of the 4th century it even took on a variation in form: its façade was divided into two superimposed registers (B).

The Biblical scenes on the front of these sarcophagi were chosen to

(B) Sarcophagus with scenes from the Old and New Testaments, about 330 A. D.
*Rome, Lateran Mus.*

fit in with the structural form. For instance, scenes of the raising of Lazarus and the miracle of Moses striking water were placed at the corners, since the dead man's sepulcher and the rock from which the water gushes forth make extremely strong, solid focal points, highly suitable for accentuating the corners (c). Later, the friezes of these sarcophagi were broken at the center by a large oval, carved with the figures of the deceased. Then scenes flanking the central figures were chosen so that they made the best use of the angles formed by the outward curve of the central medallion. Usually they depicted Moses receiving the Tablets of the Law and Abraham offering his sacrifice, because in each case the Hand of God that appears from the clouds at the top is a particularly suitable device for filling up the triangular spaces.

(c) The Raising of Lazarus: from sarcophagus of about 330 A. D.
*Rome, Lateran Mus.*

The point most worthy of note about these sarcophagi is their style. When compared to what was understood by *relief* in the previous period, it is evident that there has been a radical change. The former's rounded, plastic form has been replaced by a hard, sharp, angular form, and the delicate softly-shaded effect has given way to dramatic contrasts of light and shadow. These contrasts were obtained by long, sweeping strokes of the chisel which the sculptor used to render folds instead of modeling them.

With this negative method of working in marble, there were no longer tactile effects, but only optical. Again, in the faces of individual figures there is a stylization stemming from a real desire for self-expression caused by an inner, almost unconscious impulse.

However, side by side with this negative treatment of organic form, was another technique that aimed at a naturalistic vision through a return to plasticity and a softer, painterly approach. This movement toward a classical renaissance reached its climax toward the middle of the 4th century, and continued in the decades immediately following. A fine example, dated 359, of great artistic value, is the sarcophagus of Junius Bassus, the Prefect of Rome (p. 60 A).

Its figures are free from all schematization; they are tastefully distributed at intervals and brought to life by a slow ripple of movement, which also gives them a graceful bearing. Their clothes cling lightly to their bodies, revealing the human form beneath, and their faces assume a new expression that seems to radiate a truly unshakeable serenity.

The Junius Bassus sarcophagus has its façade divided by colonnettes into many niches, as did many other sarcophagi in the second half of the 4th century. This rhythmical partitioning halts any narrative continuity because the individual scenes are completely isolated from each other. Occasionally, these divisions are made by tree trunks instead of columns, and the spreading leafy branches of the trees form excellent arcades.

(A) Junius Bassus sarcophagus, 359 A. D.
*Rome, Vatican Grotto*

Toward the end of the 4th century and at the beginning of the 5th, we find sarcophagi showing the miracle of Bethesda and the crossing of the Red Sea (possibly derived from illuminated manuscripts). We also find sarcophagi carved to represent *Christ Enthroned in Majesty*, or *St. Peter Receiving the Law*, often against a background of a city wall. These almost certainly derive from the decoration on monuments. The mosaics in the basilica apses might have had similar origins.

At this period the strigated sarcophagus returned to fashion. It was produced chiefly at Arles in Provence, Tarragona in Spain, and later in Aquitaine in France.

At Ravenna, in the 5th century and later, sarcophagi were decorated on all four sides, and the façades were terminated at either end by colonnettes or small pilasters. Not many figures were incorporated, and they were spaced out considerably. Instead of being flat, the covers had two sloping sides like a roof, or were semi-cylindrical (B, C).

The decorations include scenes from the Old and New Testaments: images of Christ among the Apostles; allegorical designs, generally portraying sheep ranged either side of a cross or a monogram of Christ, or peacocks symbolizing immortality, surrounded by a design of plants and foliage.

From the stylistic point of view, the Ravenna sarcophagi, which really stand in a class apart, are impressive for the refined elegance of their carved figures, the depth of their modeling, and their characteristic calm and dignity.

Although Ravenna was a center of art producing works influenced by Byzantine style, it is convenient to treat the city as being in the continuing tradition of the western empire. For the sake of convenience also, strict chronological sequence is broken by treating Byzantium and the eastern empire as an entity.

(B) Sarcophagus (detail) 7th century
*Ravenna, S. Apollinare in Classe*

(C) Sarcophagus, 7th century
*Ravenna, S. Apollinare in Classe*

CHAPTER 3

# THE EASTERN ROMAN EMPIRE

(A) Sancta Sophia, 532-537
*Istanbul (Constantinople)*

In the 4th century Constantinople had not yet acquired the prestige it later attained. Founded in about 330, it was only one of several administrative centers of the Roman Empire. After the sack of Rome in 410 by Alaric, however, it became the rock on which the Christian Empire of the east rested. Thus it was in the east that the Roman Empire survived, among a predominantly Greek-speaking population, while the western provinces collapsed under the barbarians.

The art of the eastern Roman Empire henceforward developed a quite separate style from that of western Europe.

## Byzantine style

Though the character of the developed Byzantine style is quite distinct, there has been some disagreement over the date at which the term should first become applicable. It is possible to suggest that the changes in style that distinguish Byzantine from classical or early Christian art are to be discerned soon after the year 330, when Constantine marked his conversion to Christianity by transferring the capital from Rome to the ancient city of Byzantium at the end of

(B) Sancta Sophia, 532-537
*Istanbul (Constantinople)*

the Bosphorus. The city thereafter took the name of Constantinople (modern Istanbul), though the name of the old city lived on to designate the art and civilization that developed there under Christian and imperial patronage. It is equally possible to assert that there was nothing distinctively Byzantine about the art until the time of the Emperor Justinian (527-565), who was one of the foremost patrons of the new style. The numerous works for which he was responsible, like the Church of San Vitale at Ravenna, that of St. Sergius and St. Bacchus at Constantinople, or most of all, the great Cathedral of Sancta Sophia there (A, B), are indeed in a very distinct and wholly new style, not only in their architecture but also in their interior decoration, whether in sculpture, mosaic, or paint. The use of arches, of vaults, and, most of all, of the dome as units of construction, the stylized ornament, and the figures in the mosaics and paintings, all serve to distinguish the monuments of this period from those of the classical world. In actual fact, however, these stylistic changes had appeared earlier in a fairly developed form, and had already made a good deal of progress by the end of the 5th century.

Such a work as the lovely Barberini ivory in the Louvre (C), which dates from about 500, is thus just as much Byzantine as classical. It probably represents the Emperor Anastasius I (491-518). The high relief and naturalism of the portrait attest the classical heritage, but the frontal pose and rather stylized character of the bust of Christ above are in a quite distinct style, formal, even abstract, in character. This same stylization is also evident in a more exaggerated degree in the groups of Justinian and Theodora in San Vitale, Ravenna (p. 191), but the beardless youthful Christ in the apse is much more classical and contrasts sharply with that of the awesome bearded figure in the Church of St. Cosmas and St. Damian in Rome (p. 190). And the most Byzantine of all the Ravenna mosaics are those on the lowest tier of the decoration of San Apollinare Nuovo (D).

(C) The Barberini Ivory, about 500
*Paris, Louvre*

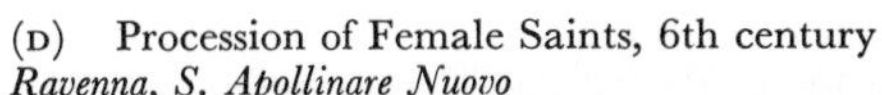

(D) Procession of Female Saints, 6th century
*Ravenna, S. Apollinare Nuovo*

(A) Monastery of St. Catherine, 6th century and later
*Mount Sinai, Egypt*

(B, C) Church of St. Demetrius
*Salonika, Greece*

## Icons and the Iconoclast Age

However fine the mosaics at Ravenna, it must be remembered that the city was no more than a provincial center. Cities in the east, like Salonika, were more important, and though the mosaics that are preserved there are very fragmentary, they are all of high quality. The finest are those in the Church of St. George, which are probably to be dated to the early 5th century (p. 193).

But Constantinople was the capital, and the best artists would certainly have been employed there. Unfortunately, however, virtually no large-scale mosaics or wall paintings survive there from this period, for any figural decoration that existed was destroyed during the time known as the Iconoclast Age. It lasted from 730 to 787 and again from 815 to 843. During that time the depiction of the divine or saintly form was prohibited by law. The movement was in a way akin to that of the Puritans in the west much later. It was a reaction to the intensity of the reverence accorded in certain circles to the icon or image of Christ, the Virgin, or some particular saint, for it had come to be believed not only that the image represented a vehicle through which the original could be approached, but also that it was itself imbued with some sort of miraculous power. Originally the term icon meant portrayal; later it came to be associated with portable pictures only, and more especially with panels bearing the figure of Christ, the Virgin, a saint, or some scene from the Bible. A few such panels of the period of Justinian or slightly later survive—there is an especially important collection in the monastery of St. Catherine on Mount Sinai (A)—but examples dating from before the days of Iconoclasm are very rare. Rather more panels are known from the centuries immediately following the repeal of the ban (p. 194); but it is only from after the 14th century that any considerable number survives. This is to be attributed in part to the fact that paintings on panel are delicate and many have perished, but it is also due to the fact that icons became more and more popular as time went on.

## The Church of St. Demetrius, Salonika

The period between the death of Justinian in 565 and the imposition of the Iconoclast ban in 730, was not as important for the history of art as that of Justinian's reign, for none of his successors equaled him as a patron. But there are some fine works on a small scale that can be assigned to these centuries, more especially in the form of silver and textiles, and in the Church of St. Demetrius at Salonika there are some interesting mosaics of the 6th and 7th centuries (B, C, and p. 195). They are mostly of a votive character and depict the patron saint of the church, accompanied in every case by a donor. They escaped the ravages of the Iconoclasts, though whether because they were for a time plastered over or because they were not in the capital, it is impossible to say. The former seems more likely, for in general the ban was firmly imposed. Italy of course was not affected; it was by then no longer part of the Byzantine Empire, being under the religious jurisdiction of the Popes, opponents of Iconoclasm, rather than that of the Patriarchs of Constantinople. This difference of view was symptomatic of the relationship between the churches of east and west, which experienced continual disagreements, until the formal break, which finally separated the Orthodox and the Roman Catholic churches in 1054.

(D) Church of St. Irene, 532, showing later mosaic in apse
*Istanbul*

## The Church of St. Irene, Constantinople

One great mosaic decoration of Iconoclast times survives; a cross in the apse of St. Irene at Constantinople (p. 65), one of the finest of Justinian's domed churches. It is quite plain and simple, though the apse is bordered by quite an elaborate floral composition. Similar decorations from Iconoclast times are known to have existed in the apses of the Church of the Assumption at Nicaea and the Cathedral of Sancta Sophia at Salonika, but soon after the end of Iconoclasm (843) they were replaced by figures of the Virgin. In the former she stands full length, in the latter she is enthroned, with the Child on her knee. They were set up soon after the middle of the 9th century.

(A) The Virgin and Child, with Constantine and Justinian, 986-994
*Istanbul, Sancta Sophia*

## The end of Iconoclasm

The end of Iconoclasm was marked by considerable redecoration using figural compositions. Work started at Constantinople, in Sancta Sophia, the great cathedral of eastern Christendom. The first large-scale mosaic to be done there was apparently that in the apse, where a figure of the Virgin and Child was set, with the Archangels Michael and Gabriel before it on either side of the vault. One of these archangels survives in part (B); the other has perished; the figure of the Virgin is also well preserved. A panel that survives over the main west door was done soon after; it shows an emperor, probably Leo VI (886-912), at the feet of Christ, while a similar panel over the south door depicts Constantine and Justinian respectively presenting models of the City and the Church to the Virgin (A); it is probably to be dated to the time of Basil II (976-1025).

(B) Archangel on vault in front of apse, about 850
*Istanbul, Sancta Sophia*

## The Macedonian Renaissance

During these years the empire was ruled by a dynasty known as the Macedonian (867-1059), and the age is often referred to as that of the Macedonian Renaissance. It was a renaissance in both senses of the word, for the art of the period was of great quality and beauty, and, because the tradition had been interrupted by Iconoclasm, there was also a turning back to earlier models. This was especially so in the illustration of manuscripts. The miniatures of two outstanding books of the age show this clearly. One is usually called the *Paris Psalter* (p. 196); the other is a collection of the *Homilies of St. Gregory Nazianzus*, which was written for the Emperor Basil I (867-886) (C).

But if the illustrations of the manuscripts were often retrospective in style, the monumental decorations had much that was new. Shortly after 843 a church in the Great Palace at Constantinople was adorned with an elaborate cycle of mosaics that are described by contemporary writers as being of outstanding quality. These mosaics inaugurated a new conception of decoration. In the central dome was a figure of Christ, conceived as the Creator of all, and looking down on the church as the Almighty looked down on the world. In the apse was the Virgin; in the pendentives of the dome were four of the most intimate scenes of Christ's life; on the vaults and upper parts of the walls were other scenes; at a lower level, rows of saints. The decoration set a fashion, and its arrangement was followed in nearly all eastern churches from that time forward.

(C) The Prayer of Ezekiel: from the Homilies of St. Gregory Nazianzus, 867-886
*Paris, Bibl. Nat.* (MS. Grec. 510, f. 438 v.)

(A) The Descent into Hell, 1042-56
*Chios, Monastery of Nea Moni*

This decoration alas has perished, like so much else in Constantinople, but the mosaics of the monastery church of Hosios Lukas in Phocis (B, C) (about 1000), the monastery of Nea Moni on Chios (1042-56), and the Church of the Dormition, Daphni, near Athens (end of 11th century) follow the system initiated in the Great Palace. Those of the Nea Moni (A, and p. 197) were done under the patronage of the Emperor Constantine Monomachus (1042-56), who is depicted with the Empress Zoë on an interesting panel in Sancta Sophia (D). All the decorations are fine, but the work at Daphni is perhaps the best. Several masters must have been employed there; the scenes in the narthex are classical and rather severe; the Christ in the dome is strange and awesome, and belongs to the east rather than the west; the scenes in the pendentives—the Annunciation (p. 198), the Nativity, the Baptism, and the Transfiguration—are more delicate and intimate, yet profoundly spiritual; they represent the acme of the mid-Byzantine style, formal, hieratic, yet surprisingly beautiful. The quality of the work here surpasses that of a panel in Sancta Sophia itself done only a short time afterwards, depicting the Emperor John Comnenus, his empress Irene, and their son Alexius, and dating from about 1118.

(C) Pentecost, about 1000
*Phocis, Greece, Hosios Lukas*

(B) Church of Hosios Lukas, about 1000
*Phocis, Greece*

(D) Christ with the Emperor Constantine Monomachus and the Empress Zoë, about 1030 (the faces were altered in about 1042)
*Istanbul, Sancta Sophia*

## Byzantine style overseas

This mid-Byzantine style was carried overseas, for Byzantine craftsmen were world-famous. They worked in Russia: the mosaic decorations of Sancta Sophia at Kiev (1037-61) are essentially Byzantine, and the Russian school of painting was developed upon a Byzantine base. They worked in and around Venice, especially at Torcello (p. 199), and taught the Venetian mosaicists. They worked in Sicily, under the patronage of the Norman emperors. Some of the Sicilian work is of very high quality. The east end of the Palatine Chapel at Palermo was decorated in 1143; the apse of the cathedral of Cefalù (p. 200) about 1150; and the Church of the Martorana in Palermo in 1151; all works supervised by Greek masters. The mosaics in the nave of the Palatine Chapel, on the other hand, were done by Sicilian pupils about 1150-60 and the cathedral of Monreale partly by Greeks and partly by Sicilians about 1184 to 1200.

Except when it was under some sort of official patronage, however, work outside Constantinople was more often in paint than mosaic, for the expense of the richer material was too great, and in the monasteries the monks themselves did the work rather than employ professional artists. The most important monastic work of the period is to be found in the rock-cut chapels of Cappadocia (E). In some of

(E) Rock-cut chapels, 12th century
*Goereme, Cappadocia, Turkey*

*Mosaics and wall paintings certainly constituted the most important arts in the Byzantine world. It was an age of faith; religious art was more important than secular art, and the decoration of a church was, except perhaps during the Iconoclast period, an absolute essential without which the building was almost as incomplete as it would have been without a roof. Small objects were of immense importance also. In early times silver vessels adorned with a decoration in relief seem to have been highly prized. In the second Golden Age enamels and cabochon work came more to the fore and, as a result of the development of the cult of relics, shrines of gold or silver-gilt, richly adorned, were made to contain them* (A, B). *Similar techniques were also developed for the decoration of ecclesiastical vessels like chalices and patens* (C, D).

A

B

C

(A, B) Reliquary of the True Cross, 948-976
*Limburg, Cathedral Treasury*

(C) Chalice, 10th or 11th century
*Venice, Treasury of St. Mark*

(D) Patens decorated with silver-gilt, 10th or 11th century
*Venice, Treasury of St. Mark*

D

them non-figural decorations of the Iconoclast period were later overpainted with figures and scenes.

These monastic paintings are sometimes rather crude, yet they are always expressive and interesting, and in some cases show real ability, as in some paintings recently discovered at a place called Eski Gümush near Nigde in Asia Minor. In the Balkans the wall paintings in the Church of Sancta Sophia at Ochrid are of really exceptional quality; they were done shortly before 1050, and show how accomplished was the best work in this medium (E, F).

The first Golden Age of Byzantine art had ended with the advent of Iconoclasm in 730. What is usually termed its second Golden Age

(E) The Virgin and Child, about 1050
*Ochrid, Yugoslavia, Sancta Sophia*

(F) The Ascension, about 1050
*Ochrid, Yugoslavia, Sancta Sophia*

A

ended with the Latin conquest of Constantinople in 1204. The empire had already been much reduced in size, but its wealth was still considerable and the crusaders spoke with awe of the treasures they found in the capital. Much was destroyed, but much was also taken to the west, and is preserved in cathedral treasuries to this day. The minor arts of the age were usually extremely fine, of great richness, and of considerable importance. Some of the finest products of Byzantine art were small portable objects—enamels, jeweled book covers, woven silks, and carvings in ivory, and the western fashion of calling them works of mere craft is quite unwarranted. Byzantine art owes much of its sumptuous character to the excellence and profusion of these smaller works.

*From about the 12th century, painted panels or icons became progressively more important* (B). *But rich silks, for use as vestments or as hangings in churches, and ivories bearing religious subjects were much valued throughout. Indeed some of the finest textiles that the world has ever seen and some of the most superb ivory carvings were produced in the royal workshops at Constantinople between the 6th and the end of the 12th century* (A, C, D, E).

B

C

D

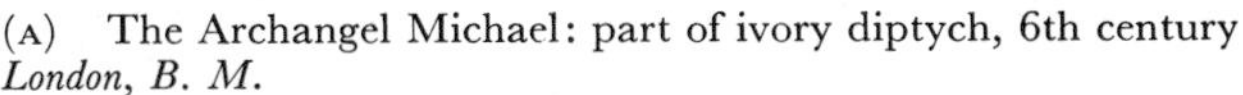

(A) The Archangel Michael: part of ivory diptych, 6th century
*London, B. M.*

(B) The Annunciation, icon from the Church of St. Clement, Ochrid, early 14th century
*Skopolje, Yugoslavia, Mus.*

(C, D) The Annunciation; and the Nativity, silk textiles, about 8th century
*Rome, Vatican*

(E) The Harbaville Triptych, ivory, 10th century
*Paris, Louvre*

(F, G) The Twelve Feasts, miniature mosaic, 14th century
*Florence, Opera del Duomo*

F

E

G

*Ivories became rare in Palaeologue times, but their place was taken by similar carvings in steatite, while from about 1350 richly bejeweled embroideries tended to take the place of the woven silks that had been so important earlier. If reliquary shrines or gospel covers in gold and enamel were beyond the resources of the state, their place was taken by miniature mosaics of the most exquisite character composed of tiny tesserae no bigger than a pin's head, set in wax* (A. and p. 73 F, G). *Beautifully illuminated manuscripts were important throughout the history of the Byzantine Empire.*

A

(A) The Annunciation, miniature mosaic, 14th century *London, V. and A.*

(B) Christ with the donor of the mosaics, Theodore Metochites, about 1310 *Istanbul, Kariye Camii*

(C) The Numbering of the People, mosaic, about 1310 *Istanbul, Kariye Camii*

(D) The Descent into Hell, wall painting, about 1305 *Istanbul, Kariye Camii*

**The Palaeologue revival**

During the Latin domination of Constantinople little was produced, but with the return of the Byzantine emperors in 1261 there began a new phase of art, usually known as the Palaeologue revival. It was distinguished by a lighter touch; the hierarchical approach that had characterized the second Golden Age gave way to greater humanism, the scenes and figures were rendered with a new interest in everyday affairs, and there was a freshness and delicacy about the work which is truly remarkable. The key monument of the style is the decoration of a small church in Constantinople, St. Saviour in Chora (B, C, D), also known by the Turkish name of Kariye Camii, for the church was turned into a mosque after the Turkish conquest in 1453. Part of its decoration is in mosaic, part in wall painting, but the styles of the two are closely similar. The mosaics were done under the patronage of a certain Theodore Metochites about 1310. It is probable that the more intimate manner evident there had begun even before the Latin conquest. A very lovely panel of the Virgin known as *Our Lady of Vladimir* (p. 201), painted in Constantinople for a Russian patron around 1125,

B

C

D

(A) The Dormition of the Virgin, about 1265
*Sopoćani, Yugoslavia, Church of the Trinity*

(B) The Deposition, 1164
*Nerezi, Yugoslavia, Church*

(C) The Virgin of Pimen, icon, 14th century
*Moscow, Tretyakov Gall.*

is intimate and tender, and there are wall paintings at Nerezi in Macedonia, done in 1164, that are just as humanist in character as the work at Kariye (B).

The most superb work in this style, however, is a mosaic in the southern gallery of Sancta Sophia at Constantinople representing the *Deësis*—Christ between the Virgin and St. John the Baptist, who intercede with Him for the sins of the world (p. 202). It is perhaps the most beautiful of all the surviving Byzantine mosaics, a work of art of the highest order. There is dispute as to whether it should be dated to the 12th or the end of the 13th century. It could not of course have been done during the Latin domination of Constantinople (1204-61), though fine paintings of the 13th century are to be found in regions where Orthodox rulers were in control, notably at Trebizond (p. 203), and in the monasteries of Mileseva (p. 204) and Sopoćani (A) in Yugoslavia, and at Boiana near Sofia in Bulgaria.

A

B

Other mosaics, from the first half of the 14th century, survive in two other churches in Constantinople, St. Mary Pammakaristos (Fetiye Camii) and St. Theodore (Kilisse Camii). There were once probably many more, but this last phase of Byzantine art is best known from paintings. A number of fine panels exist in collections in Greece, Russia, and Yugoslavia, and there are good wall paintings in Macedonia, Serbia, Bulgaria, and Greece. A number of accomplished masters, some of them Greeks and some Slavs, were working in Macedonia and Serbia from the end of the 13th century onwards, but the best paintings are at Mistra in the Peloponnesus; those in the churches of the Perebleptos (p. 205) (about 1350), and the Pantanassa (p. 206) (1428) are of outstanding beauty.

The last developments of painting on Byzantine soil took place on Mount Athos in Greece, where good, though perhaps not absolutely first class, work was done in the 16th century, and in Rumania, where some lovely decorations were produced during the same period. It was, however, to Russia that Byzantine painting bequeathed its most fruitful heritage, though it had already been absorbed into a national school soon after the middle of the 14th century (c).

C

A

## Sculpture

One of the most striking changes brought about by the development of Byzantine art had been the virtual disappearance of three-dimensional sculpture. At first imperial portraits in the Roman naturalistic style had continued to be produced, and sarcophagi were frequently adorned with sculptures in high relief depicting Christ, the Apostles, or even scenes from the Bible; there are large collections of them in Rome and Ravenna. But they should be regarded as early Christian rather than Byzantine. A change toward a more abstract approach characterized a few sculptures of the later 5th or early 6th century done in or near Constantinople, and virtually the last piece of large-scale portrait sculpture, a head at Milan usually identified as that of Justinian's empress Theodora (C), already shows a marked intrusion of the elements of the new style. These elements were at one time regarded as decadent, but today they are seen as the result of the adoption of the inward-seeking faith of Christianity and the consequent loss of interest in external appearances.

*Although religious art was always more important than secular art, good secular work was also produced, first mainly under imperial patronage and later to some extent also under that of the rich nobles. The most important of the secular works in early times were the ivories known as consular diptychs that were issued by each consul when appointed, until the office was abolished in 541 (A). From the early 6th to the late 7th century, a large series of silver vessels was produced, adorned with scenes of classical character, usually marked on the back with control stamps that date them like the hall-marks on our silver today (B). To the 10th and 11th centuries are assigned a number of beautiful ivory caskets, usually decorated with plaques of classical character. The finest of these is the Veroli casket (D).*

B

(A) Consular diptych of Rufus Germadius Orestes, consul at Rome, 530
*London, V. and A.*

(B) Atalanta and Meleager, silver plate, 613-630
*Leningrad, Hermitage*

(C) The Empress Theodora, early 6th century
*Milan, Castello Sforzesco*

(D) The Veroli Casket, late 10th century
*London, V. and A.*

C

D

(A) Heads of Apostles: from the Church of St. Mary Panachrantos, Constantinople, probably 14th century
*Istanbul, Mus. of Antiquities*

A few pieces of figural sculpture in a style similar to that of the Theodora head have been found from time to time during excavations at Constantinople. During the Iconoclast period the fashion for ornamental work in low relief was intensified, and it lived on after the ban on representation was lifted; in the second Golden Age a great many delightful tomb closure slabs were produced, decorated with geometric or stylized animal motifs. A number of typical examples are to be found built into the walls of a church at Athens known as the Little Metropolis (B); many of them are very Oriental in style and would appear to have been inspired by textiles imported from Persia or Syria. Occasionally, however, figures of Christian character were depicted, most often the Virgin; and a number of slabs survive in various collections bearing her image in low relief, usually full length with her hands raised in prayer. The finest of them, even though it is fragmentary, was found in the region of the Mangana Palace in Constantinople and is almost certainly from the 11th century (C). The fragments of an arch bearing heads of the Apostles from the Church of St. Mary Panachrantos (A), which must have belonged to an altar canopy, are probably to be dated to the 14th century, and represent a revival of sculpture in this last phase.

(B) Sculptured closure slabs, 9th century
*Athens, Little Metropolis*

(c) The Virgin Orans: from the Mangana Palace, Constantinople, 11th century
*Istanbul, Mus. of Antiquities*

*Decorations in mosaic and paint inside palaces and houses were important, but very little has survived. Attention may however be called to the floor of a court in the Great Palace of the Emperors at Constantinople that has recently been excavated* (A). *It is probably to be dated to the 6th century. From the 11th century some paintings of scenes from the circus survive at Kiev* (B), *and from the 12th may be noted some mosaics which adorn a room in the Palatine Palace at Palermo* (C). *They would seem to reproduce fairly closely those of a chamber in the Great Palace at Constantinople. Some of the textiles that survive were also no doubt intended for secular rather than religious usage. The portrait of the High Admiral Apocaucos in a manuscript of Hippocrates in the Bibliothèque Nationale, Paris, dated about 1342, serves to show how the textiles were used as a part of the secular costume* (E).

A

C

B

Though good ornamental work, some of it surprisingly classical in feeling, was produced during Palaeologue times (p. 80 A), some of the figural sculpture took the form almost of engraving on stone. A slab bearing a figure of Christ at Mistra may be noted (D). Technically speaking it can certainly be described as decadent, but it is, all the same, not without artistic merit.

It was perhaps partly because of the title Edward Gibbon chose for his great history of the Byzantine world, "The Decline and Fall of the

(A) Mosaic floor (detail) probably 6th century
*Istanbul, Great Palace of the Byzantine Emperors*

(B) Musicians, fresco on southern staircase, 11th century
*Kiev, Sancta Sophia Cathedral*

(C) Mosaic (detail) 12th century
*Palermo, Sicily, Palatine Palace*

(D) Christ, 14th century
*Mistra, Greece, Sparta Mus.*

(E) High Admiral Apocaucos: from Hippocrates Manuscript, about 1342
*Paris, Bibl. Nat.* (MS. Grec. 2144, f. 11)

D

Roman Empire," and partly because of the nature of the 19th-century outlook, that Byzantine art was for long regarded as decadent and inept. But the broadening of the horizon of vision that took place toward the end of the 19th century and the marked change of tastes in art since then have led to a new evaluation. Today there are few who would not be prepared to approve the conventions adopted by Byzantine artists, and to regard the degree of stylization and abstraction to which they had recourse as something quite normal and acceptable. Today, indeed, the great mosaic decorations of the 5th and 6th centuries, like those at Ravenna, attract as many visitors as does any great monument of classical art, while the early 14th-century

E

(A) GIOTTO The Annunciation to St. Anne, about 1305
*Padua, Arena Chapel*

wall paintings and mosaics of the little church of St. Saviour in Chora at Constantinople seem no less beautiful than the contemporary work of Giotto in the Arena Chapel at Padua (A).

But although eight centuries elapsed between the collapse of the west in the 5th century and the great father of modern painting, artistic activity in western Europe was far from negligible, either in quantity or quality. Its main energy was in architecture, sculpture, and three-dimensional works for the decoration of churches, such as reliquaries and monstrances, but there was also a continuation and development of painting in large-scale wall decoration, some mosaic, and book illustration.

CHAPTER 4

# WESTERN EUROPE TO THE ELEVENTH CENTURY

With the acceptance of Christianity as the state religion in 323 A. D., the artistic forms of expression current in the Roman Empire during the 4th century were fully accepted to serve the new religion. Just as the concept of the young Apollo in sculpture was adapted to serve as *The Good Shepherd* (B), so an impressionistic and naturalistic form of painting, which had been practiced since the 2nd century in the illustration of classical books like the Vatican Virgil (A) and in catacomb paintings (p. 86 A), was adapted for the illustration of Biblical texts.

## The Cotton Genesis

Among the earliest of such Christian books are the fragments of the so-called *Cotton Genesis* (p. 207). These fragments are all that survived the disastrous fire of 1731 in the library of Sir Robert Cotton, the great English 16th-century bibliophile whose collection became part of the British Museum in 1753. In spite of the mutilation, one can still recognize in these fragments the fine impressionistic style of painting current in 4th-century Rome. The figures are fully realized in the

(A) Illustration from the Vatican Virgil, 4th century A. D.
*Rome, Vatican, Bibl. Apostolica* (Lat. MS. 3225, f. 18v.)

(B) The Good Shepherd, mid-3rd century A. D.
*Rome, Lateran Mus.*

(A) The Good Shepherd, 4th century A. D.
*Rome, Giordani Catacomb*

round, in gentle rhythmic naturalism painted with delicate highlights. They give a vivid sense of movement, against the soft and merged colors of the background, suggesting infinite depth by the use of aerial perspective. The text of the *Cotton Genesis* is in Greek, and it was in the eastern capital of the Roman Empire, Constantinople, that this naturalistic, classical style of painting survived into the Middle Ages.

## Barbarian art

In the west, after the final collapse of the western Roman Empire in the 5th century due to internal weakness and the ever-increasing invasions of the barbaric tribes of northern and eastern Europe, the forms of expression were to undergo fundamental changes of style. The barbarians had developed arts of a quite different character from the humanism of the Mediterranean. The representation of the figure was rare, and their major art was in metalwork and goldsmith's work. On their personal belongings, their weapons, their buckles, their brooches and other jewelry, they lavished quite outstanding ability

(B) Gold buckle: from Sutton Hoo Treasure, 7th century
*London, B. M.*

(C) Helmet and sword from Vendel, early 7th century
*Stockholm, State Historical Mus.*

as craftsmen (A, B, C, and p. 87 B, C). The naturalism of the Mediterranean cultures was foreign to them, and the patterns they evolved were mainly based on an abstract and powerful use of animal forms, some fragmented and re-assembled in rich all-over patterns, others stretched and elongated into snake-like beasts intricately interlaced.

The influence of Mediterranean traditions persisted through the monasteries of western Europe that were created in ever-increasing numbers, after the foundation of monastic ideals by the Desert Fathers in Syria and Egypt. Rare survivals of the style reflecting these

A

B

C

(A) Harlton Brooch, 6th century
*Cambridge, England, Mus. of Archeology and Ethnology*

(B) Crundale sword pommel, 7th century
*London, B. M.*

(C) Purse: from Sutton Hoo Treasure, 7th century
*London, B. M.*

traditions, still basically humanist in approach but cut off from its source of inspiration and showing signs of a serious decline in ability, are the *St. Augustine Gospels*, painted in Canterbury in the late 6th century (p. 208), and the *Ashburnham Pentateuch* (p. 209), probably painted in Visigothic Spain in the 7th century.

**Northumbria**

The art and culture of Northumbria in northeast Britain was of far more significance because it was both intrinsically creative and had a great influence on the revival of learning in the whole of western Europe. It was centered mainly in the Hiberno-Saxon monasteries of Lindisfarne, the home of St. Cuthbert, and Monkwearmouth, and Jarrow, the home of the Venerable Bede, probably the foremost historian of the so-called Dark Ages. In these monasteries, contact with the Mediterranean tradition was re-established—a tradition which must have survived to some extent in Rome and especially in the south of Italy in the monastery founded by the Roman scholar Cassiodorus in the 6th century. The immediate effect of this contact was the astonishingly able copy of a Late Antique manuscript produced at Monkwearmouth, about the year 700, to be given as a present to the pope in Rome, and surviving as the *Codex Amiatinus* in the Laurentian Library at Florence (p. 90 B). Here much of the naturalism, the lively painterly technique, and the pictorial depth of the Late Antique has been fully understood. In the two finest of the large series of stone crosses erected in the 7th and 8th century in North Britain, the same fidelity to the Late Antique style can be seen (D, and p. 90 A). These perhaps somewhat academic achievements are overshadowed by the sheer creative ability of the *scriptorium* of the holy island, Lindisfarne. Here a full synthesis was achieved between the humanist Mediterranean tradition and the indigenous art of the northern barbarians. The naturalism of the classical world is not merely imitated, but fully absorbed and used as a basis for the creation of flat, abstract images fully in harmony with the flat, abstract animal art used in the manuscripts. Before the introduction of these Mediterranean models, the representation of the human figure suffered the same abstract treatment. In the *Book of Durrow*, painted probably at Lindisfarne in the second half of the 7th century, the portrait of the Evangelist St. Matthew (p. 210) shows clearly the adaptation of insular goldsmith techniques to the illumination of books. The figure is like a belt-buckle to which a head and feet have been attached.

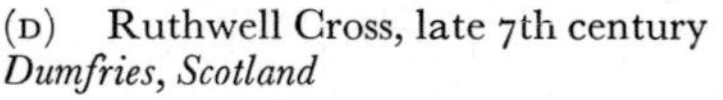

(D) Ruthwell Cross, late 7th century
*Dumfries, Scotland*

*The influence of the goldsmiths of the time, perhaps the outstanding artists of the period, is seen clearly in the decorative or "carpet" pages of the* Book of Durrow (D). *The magnificent gold shoulder clasp from Sutton Hoo* (E) *with its inlaid garnets, checkered millefiori glass, and interlace border is an example of the type of art imitated by the painter on the* Book of Durrow *page.*

A

B

(A) Christ Treading the Beasts: from Bewcastle Cross, late 7th century
*Bewcastle, Cumberland, England*

(B) The Prophet Ezra: from the Codex Amiatinus, about 700
*Florence, Bibl. Laurenciana* (Amiatino, f. Vr.)

(C) St. Matthew: from the Lindisfarne Gospels, early 8th century
*London, B. M.* (MS. Cotton Nero D. IV, f. 25v.)

(D) Ornamental page: from the Book of Durrow, second half of the 7th century
*Dublin, Trinity College Library* (MS. 57, f. iv)

(E) Half-shoulder clasp: from Sutton Hoo Treasure, 7th century
*London, B. M.*

C

D

E

**The Lindisfarne Gospels**

The masterpiece of the *scriptorium* is undoubtedly the *Lindisfarne Gospels.* The portrait of the evangelist, at the beginning of the Gospel according to St. Matthew (C) is clearly related in design to the figure of Ezra in the *Codex Amiatinus* (B). But the Lindisfarne evangelist only accepts from Mediterranean tradition the appearance of an author-portrait at the beginning of the text, as had been customary in Roman books; he makes no use of depth of pictorial form, constructed and rounded into three dimensions. The figure itself has been flattened and made into a linear pattern on the surface of the vellum, and no attempt is made to create any illusion of depth—the page is inviolate.

On the decorative pages and on the ornament lavished on the beginning of the text (p. 211), the same artistic principles are at work, but here they are based on the repertoire of northern barbaric, Hiberno-Saxon animal patterns and decorative forms, which for the most part derive from the 6th- and 7th-century metalwork of the Anglo-Saxon invaders and the Romano-Celtic and Irish Celtic peoples. The great achievement of Northumbrian artists of the late 7th and early 8th centuries is this great synthesis of a variety of aesthetic criteria. A late form of this enriched insular style is to be found in the *Book of Kells* (A).

A

C

B

## Charlemagne

While the Hiberno-Saxon monasteries of the north were creating artistic and cultural centers of European importance, the expanding and growing kingdom of the Franks in Roman Gaul was passing from the hands of the hereditary royal line of the Merovingians into the hands of the mayors of the palace of the Arnulfian and Carolingian dynasty. During the 8th century, Anglo-Saxon missionaries, the greatest among them St. Boniface, the Apostle of the Germans, were called on by the Frankish rulers to reform the Frankish church and carry the gospels to the newly conquered areas east of the Rhine.

The growing political power of the Franks enabled them at last to take over the artistic and cultural leadership of western Europe as well. When Charlemagne became king of the Franks in 768, the artistic products of the monasteries within his kingdom were still little more than pastiches of eastern Mediterranean monastic arts, basically sub-Roman in inspiration. A typical manuscript of this kind is the *Galasian Sacramentary* probably written at St. Denis, near Paris, about the middle of the 8th century, now in the Vatican Library (C). Though colorful, decorative, and curiously civilized in its apparent ease of execution, this style of painting could not play the part that Charlemagne desired in the revival of an imperial culture that he fostered at his court. It lacked the imperial grandeur, the dignity, and sheer richness which he had seen in the imperial art of the past in Ravenna, Milan, and Rome, and which he had decided should adorn his palace at Aachen—the "Second Rome" as a contemporary poet called it (B).

D

## The Godescalc Gospels and the Court School

The earliest attempt in the new style to have survived is the *Godescalc Gospels*, written between 781 and 783 for the emperor himself by the scribe Godescalc. In the picture of the seated Christ (p. 212), 8th-century insular ornament is seen in the decorative frames, combined with Italian painterly qualities that can be found in the wall paintings in north Italy of this time (D). All this is cast into a somber, heavy, and rich mold, entirely in keeping with the concepts of imperial dignity so clearly expressed in the eastern Emperor Justinian's imperial art at Ravenna. This court style was further developed in a series of manuscripts closely connected with Charlemagne himself, which used to be called the Ada Group, named after a manuscript given by Ada, who is thought to have been a half-sister to Charlemagne, to the monastery of St. Maximin at Trier. This group of manuscripts is now generally called the Court School (p. 213). In this group, all the incipient qualities of the Godescalc manuscript were fully exploited, and an imposing effect of rich, imperial splendor is given not only to the evangelist

(A) Illuminated Initial: from the Book of Kells, 760-820
*Dublin, Trinity College Library* (MS. A. 1. 6, f. 34v.)

(B) Aachen, Palace Chapel, about 800

(C) Decorated page: from the Galasian Sacramentary, mid-8th century
*Rome, Vatican, Bibl. Apostolica* (Reg. Lat. 316, f. 132r.)

(D) Wall painting, 8th century
*Cividale del Friuli, Italy*

portraits but throughout the manuscripts, with decorated initials at the beginning of the gospels, and with each page of the text written in gold and surrounded by highly decorated borders.

*The court style is also known in a number of ivory carvings, some closely associated with the manuscripts of the Court School. Perhaps the most magnificent of the carvings are the two ivory book covers that decorated the* Lorsch Gospels, *one of the manuscripts of the group. One of the covers is now in the Vatican, the other in the Victoria and Albert Museum, London* (A).

*Just as in the case of the manuscripts, the inspiration of this style seems to have come from northern Italy; the 6th-century throne of Maximian* (B, C) *illustrates clearly the kind of carvings the sculptors at Charlemagne's court were trying to emulate.*

(A) Ivory cover of the Lorsch Gospels, early 9th century
*London, V. and A.*

(B) Ivory throne of St. Maximian (detail) mid-6th century
*Ravenna, Archbishop's Palace Mus.*

(C) Ivory throne of St. Maximian, mid-6th century
*Ravenna, Archbishop's Palace Mus.*

### The Coronation Gospels

After the coronation of Charlemagne by Pope Leo III as emperor in Rome on Christmas Day of the year 800, and probably only toward the end of the emperor's life, yet another style of manuscript illumination was introduced at the court. It differs completely from the earlier style. Where the painters of the Court School had created an art out of a variety of sources, the artist who painted the evangelist portraits in the so-called *Coronation Gospels* (p. 96 A) was working in a style that shows a complete understanding of Late Antique traditions and methods. On pages of vellum stained purple, as in Greek manuscripts of the early Christian period, the author-portraits are painted in a loose, painterly, and impressionistic technique, with flickering touches of highlights, set against brooding and ominous landscapes, breaking through the pages in the full pictorial depth of antique naturalism. This style is as imperial as that of the Court School manuscripts in its dignity and splendor, and also because of its association with the Roman past. It must indeed have appealed to Charlemagne and the scholars at his court in their quest for the renewal of the empire.

A

The appearance of this style at Aachen is still something of a mystery. In the *Coronation Gospels* the name Demetrius appears written in gold in the margin, and it may well be taken as evidence that the painter was a Greek. Charlemagne's association with the Empress Irene, who ruled in Constantinople from 797 to 802, was especially close, and an embassy sent by her arrived at Aachen in 802, shortly before she was deposed. Perhaps the full vigor of Late Antique painting was still known and practiced in the conservative Byzantine court at the end of the 8th century. If so, it is possible that a Greek artist traveled with Irene's delegation in 802, or that the re-imposition of Iconoclasm—the prohibition of religious art in the Byzantine Empire decribed in the previous chapter—may have encouraged Greek artists to leave Constantinople for the more liberal atmosphere of the new western empire. Much of this is still in dispute, but the appearance in the west of a survival, or a revival, of a full Late Antique naturalism is of the greatest importance, not only as evidence of the realization of a Carolingian Renaissance under Charlemagne, but also as an overpowering influence on the art of the succeeding reign, that of Charlemagne's son Louis the Pious, and beyond it into the 10th century.

## Louis the Pious

It has often been said that the Carolingian Empire created by Charlemagne, politically by physical expansion and culturally by self-conscious personal effort, collapsed on his death in 814. It is true that Louis the Pious did not continue the process of expansion, although he did succeed in some consolidation of the eastern borders. But Louis had inherited enough wealth from his father to maintain an undivided empire under his personal rule in a period when wealth established the right to rule. It was only after Louis's death in 840 that Charlemagne's structure of a single western empire was destroyed. Louis also continued the work of his father in cultural and artistic patronage; his character and interests, however, differed greatly. The imperial grandeur which Charlemagne had successfully created were not to his taste. Louis was a more scholarly man to whom history has rightly given the appellation "the Pious."

## The Ebbo Gospels

Undoubtedly the most important manuscripts written and illuminated during Louis's reign are those usually attributed to the school of Reims, because an important manuscript in the style, the *Ebbo Gospels* (p. 214), was written at the Abbey of Hautvilliers, some 30 miles from Reims, by the Abbot Peter. It was dedicated to Archbishop Ebbo of

(A) St. Matthew: from the Coronation Gospels, early 9th century
*Vienna, Schatzkammer* (Reichsevangeliar f. 15v.)

Reims, half-brother of the Emperor Louis. The painterly style of this manuscript is undoubtedly derived from the Late Antique art of the *Coronation Gospels*. But instead of using this impressionistic technique to create a massive, calm, humanist author-portrait in the classical tradition, Abbot Peter has given us in the *Ebbo Gospels* a visionary apostle, inspired by a divine tempest to write the Holy Gospel.

*The strong feeling for revival at the court of Louis the Pious is particularly well illustrated by the striking panel in the Liverpool Museum* (A), *which in its lower part, depicting the three Marys at the Tomb, exactly copies a 4th-century early Christian carving* (C). *Ivory carvings were closely related to the manuscript styles.*

*Similarly, the lively style of the* Utrecht Psalter *is also found in a group of ivory carvings that follow closely not only the style, but the iconography of the psalter* (D, E).

A

B

## The Utrecht Psalter

The excited, linear style of the *Ebbo Gospels*, its heightened naturalism and its expressive forms, are also found in the *Utrecht Psalter* (B). This psalter is written in classical rustic capitals, and is accompanied by brown ink drawings giving a kind of running commentary to the text The continuous narrative reminds one of the classical, rotulus form, in which scene follows scene, almost in the manner of a modern strip cartoon. Intensive study of the psalter in recent years seems to emphasize the originality of the manuscript and to weaken the view that it was a Carolingian copy or an adaptation of earlier psalter illustrations. Wherever the psalter may have been illuminated, it reflects scholarly atmosphere and a truly classical influence embodied in its style of drawing and script, which would seem to be totally in keeping with the imperial patronage of the Emperor Louis the Pious.

(A) The Crucifixion, ivory panel, about 830
*Liverpool, England, City Mus.*

(B) Psalm 149: from the Utrecht Psalter, about 830
*Utrecht, University Library* (MS. 32, f. 83r.)

(C) The Three Marys at the Tomb, ivory panel, 4th century A. D.
*Munich, Bayerisches Nationalmus.*

(D) Illustration to Psalm 24 based on the Utrecht Psalter, 9th century, ivory
*Zurich, Schweizer Landesmus.*

(E) Illustration to Psalm 26 based on the Utrecht Psalter, 9th century, ivory
*Zurich, Schweizer Landesmus.*

C

D

E

(A) Gold cover of the Codex Aureus, about 870
*Munich, Bayerische Staatsbibl.* (Bibl. Lat. 14000)

(B) Charles the Bald Enthroned: from the Codex Aureus, about 870
*Munich, Bayerische Staatsbibl.* (Bibl. Lat. 14000, f. 5v.)

(C) Initial (D) for Sunday: from the Drogo Sacramentary, about 842
*Paris, Bibl. Nat.* (MS. Lat. 9428, f. 87v.)

(D) METZ SCHOOL Ivory book cover mid-9th century
*Paris, Bibl. Nat.* (MS. Lat. 9383)

## Division of the empire

With the Treaty of Verdun in 843, the Carolingian empire was divided into three kingdoms for the three sons of Louis; that of the west under Charles the Bald, that of the east under Louis the German, and a central strip from the Netherlands to Italy under Lothair I, who also received, as the eldest brother, the title of emperor. But little more than the imperial title survived this division. The centralized power of Charlemagne and Louis, and with it the centralized patronage of imperial schools, were inevitably replaced by a variety of centers in each of the kingdoms. Outstanding among them were the royal scriptoria of Charles the Bald, perhaps at the Abbey of St. Denis near Paris, of which the king was a lay abbot, and at Metz, under the patronage of Lothair I and his son Lothair II.

A

B

## The Codex Aureus

The *Codex Aureus* of St. Emmeran was a gospel book illuminated for Charles the Bald by the brothers Beringar and Liuthard about 870 (A, B). Much of the scholarly simplicity and religious intensity of the style of the time of Louis the Pious is replaced by some of the rich grandeur which had been sought by Charlemagne earlier in the century. In fact, the canon tables at the beginning of the *Codex Aureus* are copied closely from one of the manuscripts from Charlemagne's court scriptorium. But in spite of this return to imperial splendor, the unmistakable influence of the lively drawing of the *Utrecht Psalter* style is also discernible.

## The Metz School

At Metz, this same sense of movement is also to be found in the *Drogo Sacramentary*, though there is a more profound understanding of the play of rapid brush strokes, used to such effect in the *Ebbo Gospels*. The colors are lighter in hue, and the use of figure scenes enclosed in initials constructed out of tendrils of heavy, fleshy acanthus foliage gives a new form to the historiated initial (C). This new form was to play an important part in the decoration of medieval manuscripts ever after. With these books, Carolingian illumination had laid all the important foundations on which the illuminators of the 10th and 11th century were to build their styles.

C

D

(A) Ivory with two angels, about 1000
*Winchester, England, City Mus.*

## The Winchester School

Perhaps the closest links with the Carolingian tradition of the previous century are to be found in English 10th-century painting. The school in which these links are most obvious has been called the Winchester School. Although there is no doubt that this style was used at both the Old and the New Minster of Winchester, and perhaps even first developed there, it was by no means exclusively in use at Winchester. Some of the manuscripts of the school have been shown to have been produced in East Anglia and perhaps even in Northumbria, and it is more correct to call it the Winchester style.

(B) Flying Angel, late 10th century, stone carving
*Bradford-on-Avon, England, Church of St. Laurence*

## The Benedictional of St. Ethelwold

The most important manuscript in the style is undoubtedly the *Benedictional of St. Ethelwold* (p. 215), written about 980 for Bishop Ethelwold of Winchester. He was one of the churchmen who, under King Edgar, had initiated the great monastic reform movement, which gave a background of stability and scholarship for the renewed artistic activity in England after the Danish invasions of the 9th century.

The Carolingian influence that can be seen in the *Benedictional* was certainly not new in England about 980. In the embroidered stole of St. Cuthbert made by Queen Ælflaed for Bishop Frithstan of Winchester between 909 and 916 (C), and later given by King Æthelstan to the shrine of St. Cuthbert at Durham, there appears the fleshy, heavy acanthus foliage and the main elements of the figure style of the Metz

*Ivory carvings, like the little triangular piece found in Winchester* (A)*, and even major stone sculpture, like the angels in the Saxon church at Bradford-on-Avon* (B)*, clearly testify to the immense and wide-spread popularity of the Winchester style.*

(c) Embroidered stole of St. Cuthbert, 909-916
*Durham, England, Cathedral*

(A) METZ SCHOOL Ivory Casket, showing The Baptism, early 10th century
*Brunswick, Herzog Anton Ulrich Mus.*

(B) Psalm 149: from the Utrecht Psalter, about 830
*Utrecht, University Library* (MS. 32, f. 83r.)

(C) Page from Eadwine Psalter, copy of Utrecht Psalter made at Canterbury, about 1145
*Cambridge, England, Trinity College Library* (MS. R. 17.1, f. 261v.)

(D) Page from London, B. M. MS. Harley 603, f. 68r., copy of Utrecht Psalter made at Canterbury, about 1000
*London, B. M.*

school, which is also fundamental to the Winchester style of the *Benedictional*. But if stylistic criteria are not sufficient, in the case of the *Benedictional*, there is additional evidence in that a number of the most important scenes in the manuscript, for example, the Annunciation, the Baptism, and the Nativity, are based line for line and figure for figure on an ivory casket from the Metz school (A). Despite resemblances between the *Drogo Sacramentary* of Metz and the *Benedictional of St. Ethelwold*, there are differences between them. The deftly sketched figures and the light colors of the Metz book may be contrasted with the more precisely drawn figures and heavier colors of the *Benedictional*. But two facts should be remembered: little survives in England to show the stages of development between the Cuthbert stole of about 910 and the Winchester book of about 980; and it is possible that there was wide knowledge of Carolingian illumination, with the

A

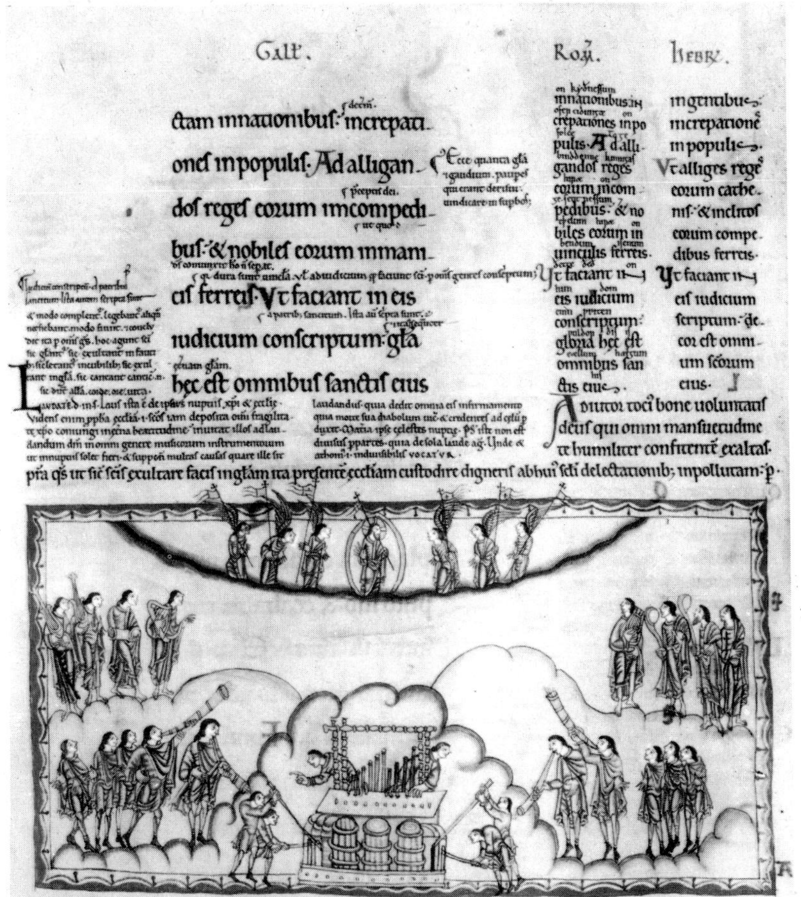

C

B

somber colors and jagged drawing of drapery of Charlemagne's Court School, in England.

Perhaps one of the most significant facts of the whole subsequent development of English art, was that sometime, probably in the later 10th century, the *Utrecht Psalter* (B) must have been brought to England. This manuscript aroused such interest that it was copied by English artists at Canterbury at least three times, first about the year 1000, and twice in the 12th century (C, D). The nervous, expressionist style of drawing seems to have had a special appeal for draftsmen in England, who since Northumbrian and even Celtic times had enjoyed the use of an expressive line. Undoubtedly it was in the pages of the *Utrecht Psalter* that the illuminators of the later Winchester style of the early 11th century found their inspiration. The figure of St. John in the *Grimbald Gospels* in the British Museum (p. 216) shows clearly the influence of the nervous elegance of the *Utrecht Psalter*.

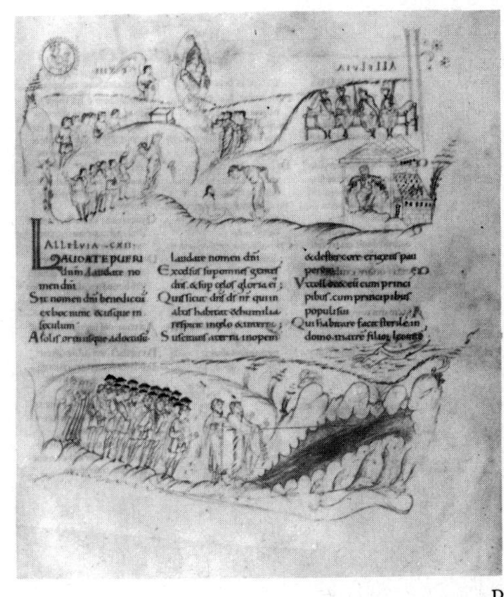

D

(A) St. Matthew: from the Gero Codex, mid-10th century
*Darmstadt, Hessische Landes-und-Hochschulbibl.* (MS. 1948, f. IV)

(B) St. Matthew: from the Lorsch Gospels, p. 26 early 9th century
*Bucharest, Nat. Library*

(C) Golden Basel Altar, 1023-24
*Paris, Mus. Cluny*

(D) Reliquary of St. Andrew's Sandal, 977-993
*Trier, Germany, Cathedral Treasury*

(E) The Golden Madonna and Child, 973-982
*Essen, Cathedral*

## Germany

While in England the heritage of Carolingian painting found such a fertile flowering, in Germany under the Ottonian dynasty, artists starting from much the same point created an entirely different style—a style that, in the final analysis, was to be of more direct and lasting significance for the further development of medieval art. One of the earliest manuscripts of this so-called Ottonian Renaissance, written toward the middle of the 10th century, was the *Gero Codex* (A). It is, in its evangelist portraits, a close copy of one of the manuscripts of Charlemagne's Court School, the *Lorsch Gospels*. But comparison between the two nevertheless reveals the change of intention, as can be seen from the Gero St. Matthew and the Lorsch St. Matthew (B). The weight of the Gero figure is greater, and it is differentiated more precisely from its background. The rich internal structure of the earlier figure is reduced in the 10th century in order to give greater

A

B

emphasis to the main outline of the figure and to the three or four main areas within it. It is this desire for greater clarity of structure and for broader, simpler patterns that underlies the artistic intentions of Ottonian painters, especially those of a school of painters closely associated with the Imperial Courts of the German Emperors Otto II, Otto III, and Henry II, of about 980 to about 1020.

C

E

D

*It is not surprising that the search for solidity in the Ottonian Renaissance is reflected in the sculpture of the period. Indeed, the rapid development of firmly modeled and well-balanced sculptural styles in all media, ivory, metalwork, and the beginnings of architectural stone sculpture, from the 10th century onwards, may well be largely the result of this desire to give weight and a firm structure to the Ottonian style.*

*Only a few examples can be shown here to illustrate the point, but we can detect in these the foundations of the Romanesque style* (C, D, E *and pp. 108-9* A *to* E).

A

B

C

(A) Bronze doors: Scenes from the Old and New Testaments, 1008-15
*Hildesheim, Cathedral*

(B) Gertrudis Portable Altar: from the Guelph Treasure, Brunswick, mid-11th century
*Cleveland, Mus. of Art, John Huntingdon Collection*

(C) Cover of Aachen Gospels, early 11th century
*Aachen, Palace Chapel Treasury*

D

E

(D) The Virgin Enthroned, ivory, 1st half of the 11th century
*Mainz, Altertums Mus.*

(E) Bishop Bernward's Crucifix, early 11th century (the base is 14th century)
*Hildesheim, Cathedral Treasury*

## The Egbert Codex

Another factor of great importance in the Ottonian school, and one on which the concept of a Renaissance in the Ottonian period is largely based, is yet another renewal of contact with Late Antique painting and with middle Byzantine iconography. This contact is very clearly reflected in a manuscript written for Archbishop Egbert of Trier about the year 980, the *Egbert Codex* (p. 217). Here all the painterly qualities of 4th-century painting are again to be seen, the light touches, the infinite background of aerial perspective. And yet the attempt to copy the style is not at all slavish nor is the manuscript painted in a technique that fully understands the classical methods, as the painter of the *Coronation Gospels* had understood them in the early 9th century. The painter of the *Egbert Codex* certainly attempts to give a pictorial image, but he goes about it in his own way; he makes use of the classical technique, he is not overwhelmed by it. His figures are clearly defined, with a strong and simple outline. The draperies make simple patterns of light and shade, and are not, as in true classical painting, broken up by them into flickering accents of light and movement.

## The Otto Gospels

In the gospels in the Aachen Treasury, probably painted for the Emperor Otto II shortly before his death in 983 (A), the same Late Antique influence is still to be seen; the same short proportions of the figure and the same little round heads of the *Egbert Codex* are in evidence. But the simple rectangular frames of the individual scenes, so clearly derived from the early model, are replaced by elaborate arches and columns of the indigenous tradition. Perhaps even more significant, the illusionistic background merging from sky to ground, still used in the *Egbert Codex*, is replaced by the abstract, simple gold background—probably taken from contemporary Byzantine manuscripts known at the court, which also provided most of the iconographic sources. In this, the tendency toward the flat, abstract simplification of forms already noticed is again advanced. The full realization of this aim is finally achieved in a gospel book probably written for the Emperor Otto III soon after his imperial coronation in Rome in 996 (p. 218). Here the emperor is enthroned and the four parts of his empire pay homage to him on the opposite page of the opening of the manuscript. Clear, simple colors and clear, simple forms dominate the page.

To illustrate the full achievement of the painters who worked for the Ottonian emperors, it would be difficult to find a finer page than the *Annunciation to the Shepherds* in a manuscript made for the Emperor

Henry II early in the 11th century (p. 219). The tension between the naturalistic representation of a scene and the abstract pictorial pattern that underlies it, is here in perfect balance.

(A) The Crucifixion: from the Otto II Gospels, p. 468, about 980
*Aachen, Cathedral Treasury*

## Regensburg and Cologne

While in the Carolingian Renaissance there had been a concentration of effort in the Court Schools, in the Ottonian period there were many other centers active alongside those patronized by the court. Among them, those of Regensburg and the Cologne area are outstanding. At

(A) St. Erhard Celebrating Mass: from the Uta Codex, early 11th century
*Munich, Bayerische Staatsbibl.*
(MS. Cod. Lat. 13601, f. 4r.)

Regensburg the rich Carolingian style of the Court School of Charles the Bald was of paramount importance. One of the finest manuscripts of the school, however, the gospel book written for the Abbess Uta of Kirchberg at Niedermünster (Regensburg) in the early 11th century, also shows the tendency toward flat abstraction in the figure drawing, in keeping with the general Ottonian direction (A). The flat pattern, however, is given a complicated structure, closely identified with an iconographic and literary commentary woven into the page, instead of the simple, purely pictorial, expression of the imperial school.

The Cologne manuscripts of the period are of a far more painterly quality and represent a totally different style, which may well be the direct result of the contemporary Byzantine influence in Germany. This was due in no small degree to Theophanus, a Byzantine princess, who had married Otto II and ruled the empire for many years during the minority of her son Otto III. Certainly the free painting, in broad and lively strokes, that characterizes the gospel book painted for the Abbess Hitda of Meschede, also in the early 11th century, has much of the classically inspired vigor, which the Macedonian Renaissance in Constantinople had developed during the 10th century (p. 220).

### The Codex Aureus of Henry III

Toward the middle of the 11th century, the Emperor Henry III (1030-56) gave a gospel book to his father's foundation at Speyer (p. 221). In this, the hard, linear style of the Court School of the early 11th century has given way to a softer, more gentle style that attempts to give weight and volume to the figures, without losing the strong pictorial structure of the earlier manner.

It is with this final phase of Ottonian art that the last of the foundations were laid on which the Romanesque period was able to build. For it was in Ottonian painting that most of the disparate elements were created, which the late 11th and 12th centuries were to synthesize into the Romanesque style—the abstract, formal, and carefully balanced forms of the court schools; the rich complexity of the iconographic themes, commentary, and thought shown in the Regensburg manuscripts; the vital, painterly qualities of a classical tradition in the school of Cologne; and the understanding of the plastic, sculptural volume of the natural world shown in the Speyer manuscript, and in the work of the goldsmiths, bronze casters, and ivory carvers. All these elements were combined and found their fullest expression in the final achievement of the early Middle Ages—the Romanesque.

CHAPTER 5

# ROMANESQUE ART

Until recently the term Romanesque was used in a wide sense to mean all the products of artistic activity in Europe between the fall of the Roman Empire and the emergence of Gothic in the 12th and 13th centuries. Today modern scholarship rightly distinguishes within those time limits a number of different styles, and Romanesque is now understood to mean the art of the 11th and 12th centuries exclusively.

Even so, it is not possible to give rigid dates for the beginning and end of the Romanesque style that would apply to all countries. In some countries, notably in Germany and England, the style of the previous epoch persisted longer than, for instance, in France; thus the Romanesque art of Germany and England started only in the second half of the 11th century. Again, in northern France and England the Gothic style was well established by the beginning of the 13th century, whereas in Italy Romanesque art continued much longer and the pure Gothic style never took root there.

Nor can it be said that there was a uniform style common to all European works of art during the 11th and 12th centuries. Regional traditions were still strong and exercised a powerful influence. Despite the unifying force of the Church, western and central Europe owed

(A) Ely, England, Cathedral, 12th century with later additions

*Like many German Romanesque churches, Worms Cathedral (B) has two choirs, at the east and west ends. Such choirs are usually flanked by towers and there are in some cases additional towers over the transepts (for instance at Mainz). The resulting appearance is one of great variety and richness, but also, due to the two choirs, of ambiguity.*

*Ely Cathedral (A) is one of the most impressive Romanesque buildings in England. The west end, ending in a second transept, suggests some inspiration from Germany.*

(B) Worms Cathedral, Germany, 12th century

*St. Stephen's Abbey at Caen* (A), *built by William the Conqueror, is one of a large series of Norman cathedrals and abbeys in which the two-tower façade is a feature. These buildings were widely imitated in Europe and especially in England after the Norman Conquest. This Norman façade was later adopted by Gothic cathedral builders in northern France and from there spread to the rest of Europe.*

(A) Caen, France, St. Stephen's Abbey, about 1065

allegiance to Rome, and east and southeast Europe to Byzantium. It was primarily in the countries linked to Rome that Romanesque art developed.

Romanesque art was not the invention of a single artist or group of artists, and it is not possible to indicate any one region where it originated. It was an art that came into being by slow development and through numerous experiments. Romanesque painting, like Romanesque architecture, was largely dependent on previous and varied traditions and emerged out of their modifications. Ottonian and Carolingian styles, and even the art of the early Christian period, exercised a powerful influence, as did the more refined art of the Byzantine east, which through political contacts, trade, and pilgrimages inspired western patrons and artists alike.

As from most of these early periods, relatively little painting has survived. There is not much chance of finding many hitherto unknown manuscripts, although well-preserved murals might still be uncovered under layers of whitewash in old buildings. We have few examples of secular Romanesque wall decoration in buildings such as castles, palaces, public buildings, or the houses of the rich. Churches, once built, usually remained unaltered for many centuries, but secular buildings were more often destroyed or underwent structural changes. Thus such Romanesque painting as is known today is found primarily in churches and is therefore chiefly, though not exclusively, religious in subject matter.

Our knowledge of the artists and craftsmen responsible for Romanesque wall paintings and manuscripts is very limited. Occasionally documents mention them, and sometimes, but only very rarely, a painter would sign a manuscript or even include a schematic self-

(B) HUGO PICTOR Self-portrait: from "Commentary by St. Jerome on the Prophet Isaiah," late 11th century
*Oxford, Bodleian Library* (MS. Bodley 717, f. 287v.)

portrait, indicating the beginning of an awareness, hitherto unknown, of the artist's importance (B). Many copyists of books and their painters were monks. This is not surprising, since the preservation of learning and the arts in the west during the Middle Ages was due chiefly to monasticism. It was in the comparative safety and seclusion of the monastic scriptoria that the practice of writing and the pursuit of learning were carried out as a form of worship. Before the emergence of the universities and the development of urban civilization monasteries were the guardians and promoters of learning and the arts.

But it would be a mistake to think that Romanesque art was exclusively monastic and that all artists were monks. There is sufficient evidence to prove that by the 12th century there was already a class of professional painters of books and murals who traveled widely in search of work. It was these men who were largely responsible for the dissemination of artistic styles and fashions throughout Europe.

*San Ambrogio, Milan* (C), *is famous mostly for its rib-vaulted interior. The exterior is traditional, with the* atrium *(forecourt) in imitation of early Christian basilicas. The free-standing* campanile *(bell tower) is also old-fashioned. The church is brick-built, but stone was used for capitals and other carved features.*

(C) Milan, S. Ambrogio, about 1100

(D) Illuminated Initial: from the Dover Bible, about 1150
*Cambridge, England, Corpus Christi College Library*
(MS. 4, f. 241v.)

This famous manuscript was written and illuminated in Christ Church, Canterbury and given to its cell, the Priory of St. Martin at Dover. The 12th-century painter and scribe are shown in secular dress.

## Wall paintings

Most Romanesque churches had large expanses of walls that were admirably suited to wall paintings, unlike Gothic buildings in which the wall space was reduced by enormous windows. The focal point of a Romanesque church was the main apse behind the high altar. Here, in the semi-dome of the apse, *Christ in Majesty* was painted, dominating the interior by its size and the hieratic pose. Frequently the opposite end of the church was painted with the Last Judgment, a composition much favored by Romanesque painters and sculptors, and, on the side walls and vaulting, scenes from the Old and New Testaments and the lives of the saints.

The aim of such paintings was two-fold: to edify the congregation and to decorate the plain walls. Awkward surfaces were often enriched with ornaments or floral design, and painting was also applied to sculptured capitals, and even carved doorways and other external features.

There was no common technique of wall painting, but fresco and tempera were employed in most important centers, and often both methods were used at once. Sometimes glazes with a base of glue were applied as well and, provided the walls were not damp, work in these media proved extremely durable.

## Italy

(A) Detail of border surrounding a fresco
late 11th century
*Rome, S. Clemente*

Italy had the longest uninterrupted tradition of church painting, and it is there that some of the most important examples of Romanesque wall paintings survive.

Rome was the leading city, and the frescoes in the lower church of San Clemente are outstanding. They were commissioned toward the end of the 11th century by the rich daughter of a butcher, and she is shown with her family in the paintings. Other surviving scenes represent episodes from the legend of the patron saint of the church, St. Clement, and of St. Alexis. According to the legend, St. Clement was martyred by being bound to an anchor, and drowned in the Black Sea. Angels built an underwater chapel over his body and the sea retired once a year to allow pilgrims to visit his tomb. On one such visit a woman left her child at the tomb by mistake and, returning a year later, found it safe and sound (B). The painting tells this story with a naïve faith and charm. The chapel, with parted curtains in the Oriental manner, and an altar with candles and the anchor, provide the background. The woman kneels to embrace her child, who tenderly stretches out its arms toward her. The mother is shown again in the same scene, but already standing and caressing her child, while a crowd of pilgrims looks on. A number of fishes around the chapel symbolize the sea. The stylized forms and arbitrary colors enhance the

(B) Episode from the legend of St. Clement, late 11th century
*Rome, S. Clemente*

impression of unreality. The exquisite arabesque borders of the scenes imitate Oriental embroidered silks, adding to the splendor and richness of the decoration (A).

Many churches in Rome at that time were decorated with mosaics, which were more durable, though more expensive to produce, than frescoes. The old St. Peter's basilica and the cathedral of Rome, St. John in Lateran, in the 12th and 13th centuries respectively, were decorated with mosaics, though no trace of them now remains. However, the mosaic apse decorations of San Clemente (1128) and of Santa Maria in Trastevere (between 1140 and 1148) still survive, and prove the Italians' mastery of this technique. Both in mosaics and frescoes, Roman masters were influenced by Byzantium.

Unfortunately no paintings survive at Monte Cassino, the celebrated monastery founded by St. Benedict, where in 1070 Abbot Desiderius sent for artists from Constantinople. But a series of wall paintings survive at Sant'Angelo in Formis, a church that was dependent on Monte Cassino, and they probably reflect the style and splendor of the mother church. These frescoes are the most complete large series preserved in Europe. They include the *Christ in Majesty* (p. 222), a large number of New Testament scenes, choirs of angels (p. 223), the Last Judgment, and the figure of Abbot Desiderius himself.

Slight variations in style indicate that several painters were employed on this decoration, but they were all strongly influenced by the Byzantine manner, for Byzantine artistic domination was strongest in the south of Italy.

Under the Norman kings, Sicily became a flourishing art center and some of the most splendid mosaic decorations in Europe are preserved there. The 12th-century mosaics of Cefalù (A), Palermo (B), and Monreale (C) are superb examples of Byzantine art on Italian soil, as are those at Torcello (p. 199), an island near Venice, and in St. Mark's in Venice. Together they were influential in spreading the Byzantine style in Europe.

The apse mosaic at Cefalù represents the gigantic bust of Christ Pantocrator, purely Greek in its iconography and style (p. 200). The

A

B

(A) Saints, 12th century
*Cefalù, Sicily, Cathedral*

(B) Detail of mosaic, 12th century
*Palermo, Sicily, Palazzo Reale, Camera di Ruggero*

(C) King William Offers a Model of the Church to the Virgin, 12th century
*Monreale, Sicily, Cathedral*

(D) St. Thomas à Becket, 12th century
*Monreale, Sicily, Cathedral*

C

only concession of the Byzantine artist who created this mosaic to the Norman patron, King Roger, is the Latin text of one page of the book held by Christ, while the other page is in Greek. However, among the scenes represented on the walls of Sicilian churches, Byzantine themes are seen side by side with hieratic figures of western saints, which include, for instance, a very early image of St. Thomas à Becket (D).

Of the numerous remains of wall painting in northern Italy, those at Galliano, near Como, are the most important (p. 224). Commissioned in 1007 by a celebrated patron of the arts and a formidable politician, Aribertus, the Archbishop of Milan, they illustrate the apocalyptic *Christ in Majesty* between prophets in the apse, and the story of St. Vincent, to whom the church is dedicated, on the nave walls. The close political links between northern Italy and the German Empire in this period explain the Ottonian stylistic influence, which can also be seen in other wall paintings, such as those at Aosta in Piedmont.

D

(A) The Martyrdom of St. Juliet: from the altar frontal of S. Quirce and S. Julita at Durro, about 1100
*Barcelona, Mus. of Catalan Art*

(B) Christ in Majesty, 1123: from the Church of St. Clement, Tahull
*Barcelona, Mus. of Catalan Art*

## Spain

The artistic styles of northern Italy were taken along the trading and pilgrim routes westward through France and into Spain where, during the 12th and early 13th centuries, wall painting flourished.

But in spite of Italian, French, and even English influences, Spanish frescoes have a distinct style of their own (A, B). Local traditions were based on Muslim art and on Christian art that existed under Arab domination in Spain, the so-called Mozarabic art. Catalonia is particularly rich in frescoes, many of which were moved with great skill, for the sake of preservation, to the Museum of Catalan Art in Barcelona. It is the region of Europe where the greatest number of altar frontals survive; they vary in quality from masterpieces to naïve works

A

B

of village craftsmen. The murals from the Church of St. Clement at Tahull (1123) (p. 121), the most celebrated series of Catalan frescoes, owe their extraordinary linear stylization of human forms to Mozarabic traditions. The frescoes of the mausoleum of the Kings of Castile and León, the so-called Panteón de los Reyes at León (about 1150) (C), display a delightful mixture of religious and secular decorative subjects painted in vivid colors against a white background.

In the royal monastery of Aragon, at Sigena (D), a series of murals, unfortunately severely damaged during the Civil War, and now removed to Barcelona, exhibit a strongly Byzantine style derived from Sicily (E). These paintings are so like some English illuminations of about 1200 that they have been attributed to English traveling painters.

(A) Crucifix (the "Volto Santo") 12th century
*Lucca, Italy, Cathedral*

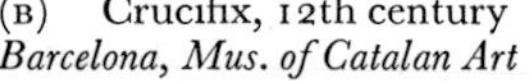

(B) Crucifix, 12th century
*Barcelona, Mus. of Catalan Art*

(C) Annunciation to the Shepherds (detail) about 1150
*León, Spain, S. Isidoro, Panteón de los Reyes*

(D) Adam and Eve Working: from Sigena Monastery, 12th century
*Barcelona, Mus. of Catalan Art*

(E) Adam and Eve Working, 12th century
*Palermo, Sicily, Palazzo Reale, Cappella Palatina*

**France**

In France, the most complete series of murals survive at Saint-Savin-sur-Gartempe, near Poitiers, dating from about 1100. They include a particularly rich series of Old Testament scenes on the barrel vault of the nave (p. 225) and Apocalyptic scenes in the porch.

The celebrated wall paintings of the Cluniac priory at Berzé-la-Ville (p. 226), which was a favored place of retreat for St. Hugh, the great Abbot of Cluny, are slightly later. The wall paintings of Cluny Abbey perished with the building, and so Berzé is particularly revealing as a reflection of the style developed in the greatest monastic center of Western Christendom. The elegant, sophisticated figures, full of Byzantine conventions, suggest that Cluny was artistically in close touch with Italo-Byzantine centers such as Monte Cassino. Certainly Abbot Hugh was a friend of Desiderius of Monte Cassino and visited his monastery.

*Comparison between the two crucifixes, the one known as the* Volto Santo *from Lucca in northern Italy* (A) *and the other from the Catalan Museum, Barcelona* (B), *shows clearly the Italian influence in Spanish sculpture during the 12th century. Similar representations of the robed Christ, deriving from Italy, are to be found in various places in Spain. The* Volto Santo *was considered miraculous, and for centuries drew pilgrims to Lucca.*

(A) Figure of Knight, 1134
*Znojmo, Czechoslovakia, Castle Chapel*

(B) Figure of Saint (detail) about 1150
*Salzburg, Austria, Nonnberg Abbey*

(C) The Tree of Jesse, after 1186
*Hildesheim, Germany, St. Michael*

(D) Crucifix (detail) (example of German Romanesque sculpture) about 1070
*Essen-Werden, Germany, Abbey Church*

(E) Figure of Saint, 12th century
*Garde, Gotland Island, Sweden, Church*

## Germany

Byzantine elements were also strong in the painting of the German Empire, especially in Austria—for example, Nonnberg Abbey at Salzburg (B) (about 1150), though few of the murals there escaped drastic restoration in the 19th century; much work has been carried out in an attempt to remove the modern additions. The flat ceiling of St. Michael's at Hildesheim (C) is celebrated for its gigantic late Romanesque representation of the Tree of Jesse, a subject invented in this period and aiming at showing the royal ancestry of Christ.

## Hungary, Bohemia, Poland, Scandinavia

Examples of Romanesque paintings, sometimes of very high quality, are found in all the countries of central and eastern Europe that adopted Christianity from Rome—Hungary, Bohemia, and Poland. The murals in the castle chapel at Znojmo (A) in Bohemia, dated 1134, combine religious subjects with the genealogy of the ruling Premysl dynasty.

A

B

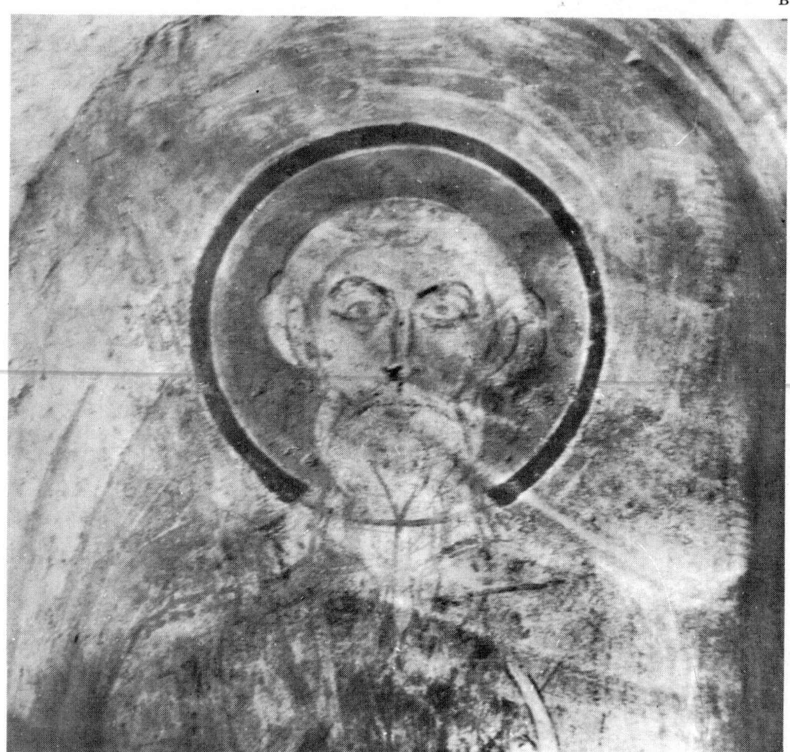

C

D

In the Scandinavian countries many murals survive. In particular those on the Baltic island of Gotland show a Byzantine influence. They are not of the type met with in other western European countries, but derived from murals in the Russian principalities such as Novgorod, with which Sweden had close commercial links. For instance, the wall paintings at Garde church exhibit not only the Russian-Byzantine style, but the saints represented seem to be eastern rather than of the Roman church (E).

E

*Smaller Romanesque churches in England were frequently constructed without an apse which, in continental churches, provides a focal point of painted decoration, usually containing* Christ in Majesty *surrounded by the Apostles and the symbols of the Evangelists.*

*In England, these subjects are of necessity placed elsewhere. At Kempley for instance Christ is on the vaulting while the Apostles are on the side walls, six on either side* (A, B).

*A similar arrangement also is found in English Romanesque sculpture as in the porch of Malmesbury Abbey. There, Christ is placed on the tympanum over the doorway, while the Apostles are on the side walls of the porch* (C, D). *Such a decorative arrangement is in complete contrast to the continental practice, where Christ and His Apostles were carved together on monumental tympana (p. 136* A*).*

## England

England suffered severe losses of her medieval mural paintings during the Reformation, but fortunately some were only covered with whitewash. Lewes Priory, the mother house of the Cluniacs in England, was pulled down; a few surviving murals in the village churches in the vicinity of Lewes, such as Hardham, Clayton, and Combes, indicate that it was an important center of painting. Another village church, Kempley in Gloucestershire (A, B) preserves some outstanding 12th-century murals, which probably reflect the style developed in the nearby abbeys of Gloucester or Tewkesbury. In the metropolitan church of England at Canterbury, interesting fragments survive from at least three different schemes. The best preserved are those in the crypt, but a single scene, that of St. Paul throwing a viper into the fire, in the chapel of St. Anselm (about 1150) (p. 227), is an example of a Byzantine style found also in contemporary English manuscripts.

Some of the best-preserved English wall paintings of the later 12th and early 13th centuries are found in France and Spain, where it is clear English artists traveled and worked. For example, at Petit-Quevilly in Normandy (E) the murals in the hunting chapel of Henry II, like those at Sigena, are obviously English work.

During the 13th century the Gothic style had begun to replace Romanesque throughout Europe. In Italy, however, Italo-Byzantine painting continued to develop without interruption, as can be seen in the mid-13th century murals in the cathedral at Anagni, which are still Romanesque in style and in spirit.

A

B

C

D

(A) Chancel, 12th century
*Kempley, England, Parish Church*

(B) Wall painting, 12th century
*Kempley, England, Parish Church*

(C) Tympanum, 12th century
*Malmesbury, England, Abbey*

(D) Porch carving, 12th century
*Malmesbury, England, Abbey*

(E) Copy of mural in Henry II's Hunting Chapel, about 1170
*Petit-Quevilly, France, St. Julien*

E

A

## Manuscript illumination

The art of book illumination, so important in the Carolingian and Ottonian periods, continued to flourish in the 11th and 12th centuries. The great wealth of material in superb condition that survives from this period permits a far more detailed study of illumination than of wall painting.

## Italy

Italy, perhaps because there was little tradition of book illumination in the pre-Romanesque period, produced fewer outstanding works than the countries north of the Alps. However, some important centers existed in Rome and Tuscany, and especially in Monte Cassino and the south. The celebrated *Exultet* scrolls (A) of southern Italy show great originality of form and style. They are large vellum scrolls with pictures and a text, and were used during the blessing of the paschal candles on Easter Saturday. The text was that of a hymn sung from the pulpit, while the pictures were seen by the congregation as the scroll was gradually unrolled. Consequently, the text and the pictures face in different directions.

B

*The amusing picture in the section of the* Exultet *scroll illustrated* (A) *mirrors the scene that the congregation was witnessing at the time it was being read: that of the priest reading an* Exultet *scroll from the pulpit. The pulpit of the Cappella Palatina, Palermo* (B), *a typical one of the Romanesque period, features many details that can be compared with the* Exultet *scroll illustration.*

## Spain

Spain, like Italy during this period, lay outside the mainstream of development. In comparison with the striking originality of the artistic achievement of the Mozarabic age, the manuscripts of the Romanesque period in Spain were rarely outstanding. Some of the large Catalan Bibles of the 11th century still show a certain richness and inventiveness, but those of the 12th century merely reflected other European styles. Elements of the Mozarabic style (C) reappeared for a while and even penetrated to France, where a copy of an Apocalypse made at Saint-Sever (D) in Gascony (about 1050), shows the great vitality this purely Spanish artistic tradition achieved.

But it was in France, England, and Germany that the greatest masterpieces of illumination were created, even if their inspiration was frequently of Byzantine origin.

C

D

(A) *Exultet* scroll (detail) late 11th century
*Pisa, Mus. Civico*

(B) Pulpit, 2nd half of the 12th century
*Palermo, Sicily, Cappella Palatina*

(C) Figures on a capital (example of Mozarabic influence in Spanish sculpture) mid-11th century
*León, Spain, Panteón de los Reyes*

(D) Page from the Apocalypse from Saint-Sever, Gascony, about 1050
*Paris, Bibl. Nat.* (MS. Lat. 8878, f. 52v.)

A

Continental elements can be traced in English sculpture as well as in book illumination. The grouping of the figures, the folds of the clothing, and the architectural setting in the relief from Chichester Cathedral (A) have a close resemblance to the biblical miniature from the St. Albans Psalter (B) since both works are strongly influenced by Ottonian art.

(A) Mary and Martha at the Gate of Bethany Kneeling before Christ and the Apostles, about 1140
*Chichester, England, Cathedral*

(B) Christ Carrying the Cross: from the St. Albans Psalter, p. 46, about 1125
*Hildesheim, Germany, Library of St. Godehard*

## England

It is generally supposed that Romanesque art was introduced to England with the Norman conquest of 1066, but in fact the first signs of the new style in architecture, sculpture, and painting made their appearance a decade earlier.

Shortly before the conquest, the exuberant style of the Winchester school of the Anglo-Saxon period gradually changed into a more restrained and structural figure-style. Once the country was occupied, the Normans started to reorganize the monasteries, appointing Norman abbots in place of English, and even bringing monks from overseas. They imported a style of illumination that was very modest and featured illuminated initials composed of foliage, "inhabited" by human or animal figures. Thus after the conquest there were two styles of book illumination: one traditional and the other Norman. A psalter in the British Museum (*Arundel 60*) contains illuminations in both styles. The scene of the Crucifixion (about 1070) (p. 228) shows the Norman Romanesque style in the linear treatment of Christ's body, but the foliage is clearly derived from the style favored by the artists of the Winchester school.

The two styles continued to exist side by side until early in the 12th century, when they fused. There are still traces of Viking elements in English illumination of this early period, and even when the actual conventions of the style finally vanished, the Viking love for transforming all human or animal forms into a complex abstract pattern survived for a long time. While the early Romanesque books in England were chiefly illuminated by initials, in the 12th century full-page pictures became more and more popular. English psalters and bibles of the 12th century are among the most sumptuous books of Romanesque times. Canterbury, Winchester, St. Albans, and Bury St. Edmunds were among the most famous of many active centers, and books were produced there not only for churches and monasteries, but also for rich and pious men and women. For instance, the *St. Albans Psalter* (B) (about 1125) was made for a woman recluse who lived nearby. The *Bury Bible* (p. 229), made about 1145 by a secular artist, Hugo, for the abbey of Bury St. Edmunds, is one of the earliest and most accomplished English books showing a strong Byzantine influence, especially in the treatment of the heads and draperies. These are of the so-called *damp-fold* type, consisting of cloaks that cling to the bodies as if they were soaked in water. The narrow folds drawn by double parallel lines indicate both the forms of the body structure underneath and provide a decorative pattern.

B

(A) Jacob's Dream: from the Lambeth Bible, mid-12th century
*London, Lambeth Palace Library* (MS. 3, f. 6)

(B) The Betrayal of Christ; and the Scourging of Christ: from the Winchester Psalter, about 1160
*London, B. M.* (MS. Cotton Nero C IV, f. 29r.)

(C) The Dormition of the Virgin: from the Winchester Psalter, about 1160
*London, B. M.* (MS. Cotton Nero C IV, f. 21r.)

(D) The York Virgin, about 1150
*York, Minster*

It is possible that the same painters occasionally were responsible for both monumental and manuscript painting, as can be seen in the similarity of style between the *Bury Bible* and the St. Paul mural at Canterbury.

The *damp-fold* style was not exclusive to Hugo's work. The large *Lambeth Bible* (A) from Canterbury and the *Winchester Psalter* (B) are two lavish books in which this convention was also used; the folds are multiplied in an extraordinary way to create a rich pattern, which, combined with the exaggerated poses and contortions of the figures, produces an effect of movement and tension.

A

B

Byzantine elements, already to be seen in the *Bury Bible*, were at their strongest in the second half of the 12th century. Byzantine works must have been taken to England, for two pages of the *Winchester Psalter* (C) contain clear copies of Greek icons or miniatures. The contacts with Sicily, too, were very close, and many Englishmen must have been familiar with the mosaics that were being made there at this time. The Crusades provided numerous opportunities for travel to Constantinople and other Greek centers. The gigantic *Winchester Bible* (p. 230), a superb book executed by a number of artists over a number

The York Virgin (D), *a sculpture deliberately damaged during the Reformation and re-used as building material, is a masterpiece full of Byzantine elements probably derived from Sicily. The Archbishop of York William was in long exile in Sicily, and many Byzantine works of art must have been brought to York on his return in 1154.* The York Virgin *could have been inspired by one such imported object.*

C

D

(A) Illustration from the Paris Psalter (copy of the Utrecht Psalter) about 1200
*Paris, Bibl. Nat.* (MS. Lat. 8846, f. 66r.)

(B) Life of Ste. Radegonde, mid-11th century
*Poitiers, France, Bibl. Municipale* (MS. 250, f. 21v.)

(C) St. Luke: from the Grimbald Gospels early 11th century
*London, B. M.* (MS. Add. 34890, f. 73v.)

of years in the second half of the 12th century, was started in the dynamic and expressive style of the *Lambeth Bible* and the *Winchester Psalter*, but gradually the Byzantine elements came to the fore. The domination of English illuminations of the late 12th and early 13th centuries by the Byzantine style became so widespread that the Romanesque style disappeared. The celebrated Carolingian *Utrecht Psalter* was copied at Canterbury at least three times, and the last copy (about 1200), now in Paris, completely abandoned the pen-drawing technique of the original, in favor of the rich palette and the Byzantine figure-style (A). All scriptoria, from Canterbury in the south to York in the north, fell under the spell of this fashion. This classicizing style, inherited by Byzantine art from antiquity, is illustrated by *The Visitation* in the *Westminster Psalter* (about 1200) (p. 231). Here all folds have their logic and are no longer a decorative device. When Gothic painting appeared in England in the first half of the 13th century, it was to displace not Romanesque but this Byzantine-inspired art.

A

**France**

The fame and prestige of English painting must have been very great, for many English books found their way to the continent, and it seems that many book illuminators went there too. This can be seen for instance on the first page of an illustrated *Life of Ste. Radegonde* (B) at

Poitiers (mid-11th century) which, if not actually the work of an English artist, closely imitates the late Winchester style (C). English artistic influences were felt particularly strongly in northern French and Flemish centers, and especially in the abbey of St. Bertin at Saint-Omer. Not only was the influence of English styles felt in northern France, but they also contributed to the creation of schools of illumination in such far-off regions as Burgundy.

Burgundy saw at this time the development of two powerful monastic orders, the Cluniacs and the Cistercians. The great age of Cluny

C

B

(A) The Commission to the Apostles, tympanum, about 1130
*Vézelay, France, La Madeleine*

(B) "Inhabited" Initial: from Saint Grégoire le Grand, Moralia In Job, 12th century
*Dijon, France, Bibl. Municipale*
(Cîteaux MS. 168-70, vol. III, f. 59)

(C) Initial from psalter written for the Abbey of Moissac, 11th century
*Oxford, Bodleian Library* (MS. d'Orville 45)

was the 11th and early 12th century. Cluniac wall painting was, as already mentioned, Italo-Byzantine in character, while Cluniac books, few of which survive, seem to have been strongly influenced by the art of Ottonian Germany. The new Cistercian order, on the other hand, through one of its most able abbots, Stephen Harding, an Englishman, established a direct contact with English art. It is generally believed that the Cistercian manuscripts from Cîteaux owe much to the Anglo-Norman style of "inhabited" initials. Some of the Cistercian initials are remarkable for the slightly satirical observation of nature and life, especially monastic life. Monks, employed on menial tasks, their habits in shreds, form the initials; their bodies, often distorted to provide the required shape of a letter, verge on caricature (B).

A

B

C

France had a great number of regional schools of Romanesque illumination. One distinct school originated in the south at Albi and Moissac (C) in the 11th century, and its influence spread north up to the Loire and even beyond. The principal motifs of the decoration of this school were fighting animals within thin interlaces, with the figures drawn in an angular, geometric style.

Limoges was an important center of illumination in which the southern and northern elements freely mixed (p. 232); but the most vital and inventive illuminations were produced in the northern regions of France, especially along the border of Flanders. In this region, fruitful interchanges of ideas had been taking place between the neighboring cultures, Anglo-Saxon, German, and French. It was a particularly prosperous and progressive part of Europe, thickly populated, and studded with important monasteries. Although most of these monasteries have disappeared, many of their libraries survive. Similar prosperity existed in what is today Belgium, and what was then Lower Lorraine, part of the German Empire. The favorable geographical position, long artistic traditions, and political and economic factors encouraged there a very lively artistic life, of which book illumination formed an important part.

*As seen earlier* (p. 126), *the tympana of continental churches, unlike those in England, are impressive monumental carvings containing many figures. One of the finest Romanesque examples in France is at Vézelay* (A)*; another notable tympanum, representing the Last Judgment is to be found at Autun.*

The abbey of St. Bertin at Saint-Omer was a center of illumination, and in its early stages (about 1000) was strongly influenced by the Winchester style. Soon, however, a more clearly Romanesque manner was evolved there, characterized by extreme angularity of the figures. This style became modified during the 12th century under the influence of Byzantine art, for Byzantine elements, with their classicizing forms, had as profound an effect on continental as on English illumination. These Byzantine elements can be detected very early in Flanders in the Mosan school, of which Liège was the chief center, for instance in the *Stavelot Bible* (1097-98), in which the art of the illuminated initial combining floral and figural motifs reached its height (p. 233). The Mosan region was celebrated for goldsmith's works and enamels, and the manuscript painting there is closely related to the art of enamel painting.

## Germany

Regional schools of illumination in Germany were extremely numerous, those in the west showing some influence from France and Flanders.

Salzburg was one of the most active centers in the south, while a number of important scriptoria in Westphalia and Saxony developed their own styles, and their influence extended to Denmark. The countries of central and eastern Europe, which had no previous traditions in manuscript illumination, made an interesting contribution to it in the Romanesque period. Bohemia adopted a style which was a variant of that in the Lower Rhineland, and Poland was strongly influenced by the art of the Mosan region.

Toward the end of the Romanesque period, an outstanding artist, whose name is not known, was active in the service of Abbot Berthold of Weingarten, near Lake Constance. Among the books illuminated by him is a missal (B) characterized by a plastic and expressive style, which as time went on became a feature of German art.

At about the same time, many centers in Germany, France, and England were abandoning the Romanesque traditions of a flat, geometric style in favor of a more naturalistic treatment of space and the volume of the human body. This was undoubtedly a result of the strong Byzantine influence and, more difficult to account for, of the influence of classical antiquity (p. 234). The true Gothic style in painting was not formulated until about the middle of the 13th century.

The style which divided the Romanesque from the Gothic is one that is usually called by the unhappy name, Transitional; though short-lived, it was in fact a style of its own.

(A) The Dormition of the Virgin, 10th century
*Cologne, Schnütgen Mus.*

*The representation of the Dormition of the Virgin in all artistic media in the west follows a set pattern introduced from Byzantine art. The Romanesque examples illustrated, from an illuminated manuscript* (B) *and a stained-glass window* (C) *are striking in their resemblance to a Byzantine ivory* (A).

(B) The Dormition of the Virgin: from the Berthold Missal, about 1200-25
*New York, Pierpont Morgan Library* (MS. 710, f. 107r.)

(C) The Dormition of the Virgin, 1220-30
*Cologne, Schnütgen Mus.*

## Stained glass

Monumental and manuscript painting of the Romanesque period was closely related to other branches of art, for instance sculpture, but a particularly close stylistic connection existed between painting and stained glass. Very few examples earlier than the middle of the 12th century survive, but after that date glass became increasingly popular. The best Romanesque glass is found in France (at Le Mans and Poitiers (A) for instance), and it was in the celebrated abbey of Saint-Denis, near Paris, that in about 1140 a series of glass windows was made which stimulated a particularly fruitful development in this field. The abbey of Saint-Denis (B) was the first Gothic building, and in the subsequent rapid development of this new style in architecture the windows became increasingly large. Chartres Cathedral (from 1155 onwards) was the next stage in this development, in which the Mosan style and iconography are believed to have played some part. Closely related to French glass is that which decorates the choir of Canterbury Cathedral, rebuilt after 1174 (p. 235). Although the inspiration here was French, the English glass retained some of the purely English stylistic features that were characteristic of such manuscripts as the *Lambeth Bible* and the *Winchester Psalter*, namely the exaggerated poses and violent movements. The Canterbury glass was, however, no longer purely Romanesque. The naturalism in the treatment of the folds was the forerunner of the 13th-century style that led eventually to Gothic.

(A) Crucifixion window, upper part, 12th century
*Poitiers, France, Cathedral*

(B) Interior of choir, 12th century
*Saint-Denis, France, Abbey*

CHAPTER 6

# GOTHIC ART

## The background of Gothic painting

The Gothic style originated in the great social and intellectual changes that took place in northern Europe in the 12th century. In the 10th and 11th centuries enclosed monastic communities had been the sole guardians of culture and of religious truth in a world of peasants and squabbling petty warleaders. In the 12th century the urban population of northern France expanded rapidly, and the prospect of prosperity bound the townspeople and nobility to the king and helped to confirm the royal power. Consequently, the government of the realm could be tackled on a new scale. Wonderful new opportunities for education were available to young men who sought advancement through their technical and intellectual skills. In addition, conscious efforts were made by popes and bishops to raise the standard of public and private conduct among the secular clergy and among lay rulers. The sustained high-seriousness and selflessness with which St. Louis (1214-70) ruled France and led Europe set the tone of public life in the 13th century, and perfectly fulfilled the promise of the 12th century. Significantly, St. Louis was one of the most active patrons of Gothic art. The Romanesque style had been evolved by artists working in the service of the old monastic communities. The Romanesque monastery turned blank barrack-like walls on the world, while on the interior, ornament was richly displayed, notably round the altar and in the cloister. The Gothic style was evolved to serve the needs of a much wider community, laymen as well as clerics. The Gothic cathedrals were as lavish outside as inside, their huge façades carrying rows of statues representing the honored heroes of Christendom and sculptured scenes setting out clearly the doctrine and history of the Christian faith (A, and p. 143). A cathedral such as Notre Dame at Chartres was the very center of the commercial and religious life of the district, and was erected both as a matter of prestige and as a corporate act of devotion, the cost being shared by bishop and chapter, king, queen, and nobility, as well as the townspeople themselves. Religion and the affairs of the world were inextricably mingled.

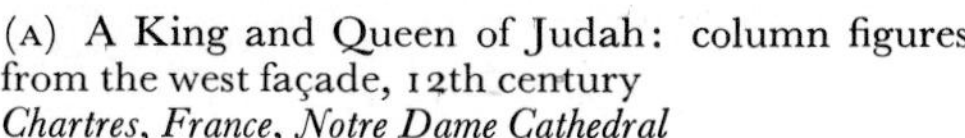

(A) A King and Queen of Judah: column figures from the west façade, 12th century
*Chartres, France, Notre Dame Cathedral*

VILLARD DE HONNECOURT Christ in Majesty: from the Notebook, about 1235
*Paris, Bibl. Nat.* (MS. Fr. 19093, f. 16v.)
This magnificent drawing reveals the dignity, confidence, and humanity of the art of the age of Faith.

North transept portals and porches,
12th century
*Chartres, France, Notre Dame Cathedral*

**Architecture and Gothic painting**

In their church designs, Gothic architects emphasized large window-spaces and the flowing rhythm of slender wall shafts and vaulting ribs, at the expense of plain wall surfaces. As a result, wall painting, without which no Romanesque church was considered complete, was exiled from churches, except in Italy, where architecture continued to be Romanesque in feeling, with large unbroken wall areas. In northern Europe painters were still employed to devise huge wall decorations, no longer in churches, but in castles and palaces, notably those of the kings of France and England. Painting, however, remained a necessary adjunct of the Gothic cathedral in two ways. Outside, the sculptured doorways originally resembled pages from a colossal illuminated manuscript, for all the figures, foliage, birds, and beasts, were vividly colored and gilded. Inside, the great windows were fitted with dazzling sheets of stained glass, designed by the best painters of the age. The sculptures of the cathedrals have long ago been scoured clean by wind and weather, but the glass remains undimmed.

### A stained-glass window at Chartres

A typical example of French Gothic stained glass is the central portion of a tall lancet window at Chartres, in which illustrations of the parable of the Good Samaritan are interwoven with a set of scenes from the history of Adam and Eve (p. 236). The figures are arranged in geometrical compartments, circles, and quatrefoils. At the bottom left, the Good Samaritan binds the head of the hunched, despondent traveler who has been assaulted by thieves in the open country between Jerusalem and Jericho. Then the wounded man, mounted on the Samaritan's horse, is led briskly toward the inn, where the innkeeper stands beside his crowded stable and stretches out his hand to take the proffered payment. In the bottom lobe of one of the quatrefoils, the Samaritan looks with anxious commiseration at the traveler, whom he has clothed and laid in a comfortable apartment. At the center of the same quatrefoil, Adam, who ultimately fell victim to an assault by the grand thief Satan and had to be rehabilitated by Christ Himself, sits, still unfallen, among the trees of Paradise. At the left, God animates Adam with the breath of His mouth. At the right, Adam lies asleep on a bank and God molds the body of Eve. In the upper compartment, God forbids Adam and Eve to eat of the fruit of the Tree of the Knowledge of Good and Evil.

Between its reading of the narrative scenes, the eye rests on the intervening panels checkered with red and blue, which radiate a wonderful flickering mauve in contrast to the strong, steady blue and red against which the figures move. The shapes of the compartments, emphasized by their thick lead frames, make a buoyant pattern of the whole window, but this pattern is not too strong for the narrative scenes. They also have a powerful rhythm. Draperies flow and billow, delicate trees sprout and sway, and the lithe figures are poised like human dragon-flies, streamlined and alert. The spectator is struck not only by the technical ingenuity with which the glass has been steeped in color and the whole elaborate jig-saw pieced together, but also by the fact that a solemn religious theme is deliberately made attractive by art.

### Manuscript illumination

No hard and fast division can be made between the artists who created the stained-glass windows of the Gothic cathedrals and the painters of the precious illuminated manuscripts of the period. The English illuminator W. de Brailes who flourished in the first half of the 13th-century and whose name we know from signatures in two of his manuscripts (A), may also have designed windows. At any rate a detached page painted by him, and now in the Fitzwilliam Museum, Cambridge, England, is strongly reminiscent of stained glass in its arrangement of the narrative scenes in rows of compartments, interrupted with flowing foliage patterns (p. 237). The figures are less graceful than those of the Good Samaritan window, but the styles of the two works are substantially similar. De Brailes's painting probably comes from a psalter, that is, from an illuminated copy of the Psalms of David, a

(A) W. DE BRAILES Signature of artist: detail from detached leaf from a psalter representing the Last Judgment, about 1230
*Cambridge, England, Fitzwilliam Mus.*

type of manuscript in great demand in the 13th century for the use of wealthy laymen. St. Louis's first reading book was a psalter, now in Leiden University Library (p. 238). These small, easily portable aids to private study and devotion are as typical of Gothic art as the enormous Bibles produced for institutional use in monasteries are typical of Romanesque. The Gothic psalter frequently contained a brief summary of Biblical history in pictures, and was deliberately designed to hold the attention of the layman, whose mind might otherwise wander, as we know Henry II of England's tended to do, during the long Latin services (A). De Brailes knew exactly what his clientèle wanted, and his work helps us to understand the nature of Gothic art. He displays the ancient scriptural narrative as a racy picture-cycle, full of psychological insight. A new realism has replaced the solemn symbolic art of the Romanesque period.

In de Brailes's picture Adam and Eve have eaten the forbidden fruit, and offer their separate explanations to God. Question and answer go back and forth on scrolls. It is comparable to the popular late-medieval mystery plays, with actors in the roles of God, Adam, and Eve. God flings clothes over the heads of the fallen pair, and they are seen earning their bread by labor. Next, Cain and Abel offer their sacrifices to God. The Book of Genesis does not state how God made it plain that he rejected Cain's sacrifice, but de Brailes cannot leave the point unsettled. The flames of Cain's bonfire curl down toward the earth, while those kindled by Abel shoot straight up to heaven. Cain turns and contemplates the back of his brother's head with purposeful malice, then he strikes him dead with an animal's jawbone, an apt symbol of primitive violence. Adam and Eve sit in the borders, lamenting the new trouble that has beset them. Next, Cain flees from the justice of God, turning his peculiarly expressive sensual face toward the accuser. Finally, Cain is disposed of by an arrow from Lamech's bow. De Brailes has an eye for the odd and telling detail. The combination in his art of a strongly secular tone with traditional religious themes is characteristic of the lively questing mentality of the 13th century.

(A) Beatus page from a psalter, early 13th century
*London, B. M.* (Landsdowne MS. 420, f. 12v.)

## Matthew Paris

The same eagerness to extend the frontiers of art is found in the work of Matthew Paris (died 1259). De Brailes was probably a secular cleric, but Paris was a monk of St. Albans Abbey near London. Despite his monastic vows, Paris was insatiably curious about men and affairs, and he compiled a history of England which he carried up to his own times (B). He illustrated his chronicle with a host of pithy drawings. The greatest English celebrity of 1255 was not a prince, or a bishop, but an elephant, which arrived at the Tower of London as a present from St. Louis to King Henry III. Of course Matthew Paris was soon on the spot to record its appearance, previously known in England only by hearsay. His tinted drawing of the great beast is typical of the Gothic style in its combination of accurate observation with an innate feeling for line and pattern (p. 239). Paris approached the elephant in a scientific spirit. He inscribes his picture with the words "From the size of the man drawn here one can get an idea of the size of the beast." But truth to nature is not pursued so far that the simple logic of the vellum page is disrupted. The elephant remains a two-dimensional pattern. There is no desire to carry the eye of the beholder into illusionary depth.

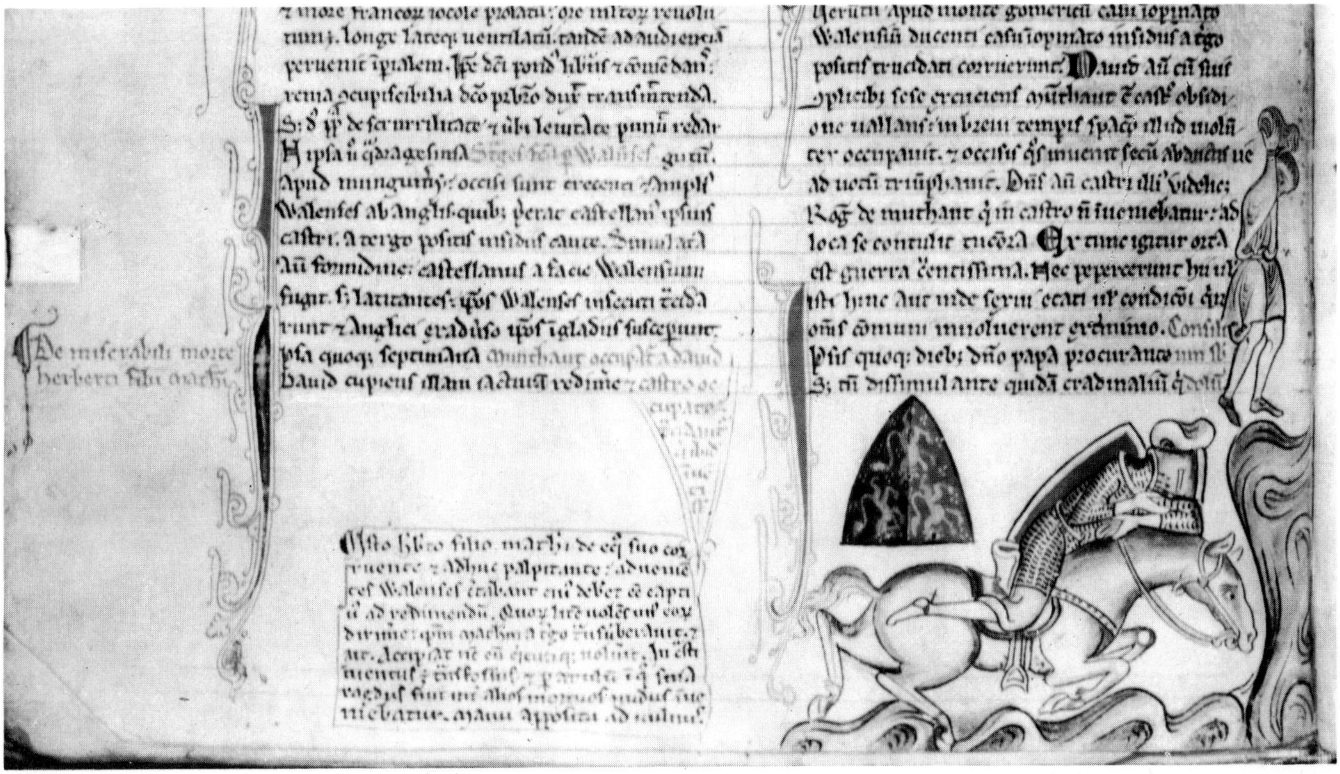

(B) MATTHEW PARIS Death of Herbert Fitz Mathew, killed by a Welshman: from "Chronica Majora," 1245
*Cambridge, England, Corpus Christi College Library* (MS. 16, f. 183v)

## Saints' lives and the illustrated Apocalypse

Paris was responsible for a remarkable series of fully illustrated lives of saints, a type of literature regarded as suitably edifying reading-matter for the lay people. Paris's *Life of St. Alban,* now in Dublin (A), has notes on the fly-leaf which show that the author-artist ran a primitive kind of lending library for the great ladies of England. He may have contributed to the astonishing popularity in 13th-century England of illustrated lives of St. John, containing in addition to his ordinary life the exotic and exciting visions from St. John's "Book of Revelation." In the 13th century the Book of Revelation was cut down to size; it was no longer, as in the Romanesque period, a terrible and frightening book, but was visualized as a religious romance, full of dragons and knights and ladies in distress, with just that touch of strangeness which made secular stories of magic and adventure so attractive to lay audiences (B). One of the most beautiful illustrated manuscripts of the Book of Revelation is the *Douce Apocalypse* in the Bodleian Library, Oxford, painted about 1270 for Henry III's son Edward. The illustration of an incident from Chapter 8 of "Revelation," when an angel blows a trumpet and part of the sun and moon and stars becomes

(A) MATTHEW PARIS Martyrdom of St. Alban: from "The Life of St. Alban," about 1240
*Dublin, Trinity College* (MS. E. i. 40, f. 38r.)

(B) Illustration to St. John's Book of Revelation, Chapter 12: from the Apocalypse Manuscript, about 1250
*Aachen, Germany, coll. Dr. Peter Ludwig*

dark, is typical of the charm, grace, and optimism of these paintings (p. 240). The elegant prancing angel plays his trumpet like a flute in a lovely landscape of shrubs and flowers. The darkening sun and moon are tucked away unalarmingly in one corner among rippling clouds. Again there is the characteristically Gothic balance between realism and surface decoration. There is just enough naturalism in the flowers and grasses and trees, just enough substance in the limbs and draperies of the angel, to satisfy an intelligent observer, but the picture makes no attempt to deceive, to pretend that it is anything but a painted page. The Romanesque style laid much less emphasis on truth to nature. The coming Renaissance style laid much more. But the attractiveness of Gothic lies in its sensitive understanding of the equal demands of visual truth and artistic truth, that is, of the laws that govern the world of natural appearances and the laws that guide the artist in the right handling of his chosen medium, whether metal or stone, glass or paint.

## Royal patrons

The Gothic style was refined and polished through the influence of secular patrons who were quick in their appreciation of beauty and lavish but discriminating in their expenditure on the arts. St. Louis's biographer, Jean de Joinville, describes the great king coming into the garden of his palace in Paris dressed in black silk and with a coronal of white peacock plumes on his head. At the king's orders, carpets were spread under the trees, on which he sat with his attendants to hear legal pleas and personally administer justice to his assembled subjects. St. Louis and his brother-in-law Henry III of England carefully designed the visual environment in which they lived. The works of art

(A) Westminster Retable (detail) 1260-70
*London, Westminster Abbey*

they commissioned have a sweetness and graciousness that reflects their own extreme cultivation of mind (p. 241). One of the most precious relics of court art of the reign of Henry III is the *Westminster Retable* in Westminster Abbey, a large painted panel divided by architectural frames (A). It contains scenes from the miracles of Christ, together with a number of full-length figures, all sadly mutilated. The best preserved is St. Peter, a tall, swaying figure voluminously draped in a mantle whose decorative border ripples down from shoulder to wrist, and from wrist to feet (p. 242). The saint's elegantly extended fingers and delicate features, and the exquisite smoothness and finesse of the whole painting, are the creations of an artist of almost feminine sensitivity.

**Secular wall painting**

The Retable proves that panel-painting was practiced in 13th-century England. The most magnificent works of painting produced for the kings of France and England must have been the wall decorations in their various palaces. Though there are literary records and a few copies of these, none of the originals has survived. Henry's famous painted chamber in the old Palace of Westminster was ornamented with all the "warlike histories" from the Old Testament, and may have been inspired by a similar royal apartment in France. A magnificent French manuscript of about 1250, called the *Maciejowski Bible* after a 17th-century Polish owner and now in New York, shows the warlike scenes of the Old Testament in just the way they must have appeared in the great royal murals. Under an architectural canopy, the camp of the king of Elam is sacked by Abraham's troops (p. 243). The ancient Israelites are accoutred in the latest fashion, and the tents through which they hurry are just like those that housed St. Louis on his crusading campaigns. In a gospel book from Mainz, of about 1260, the fall of Jerusalem and the Jews being led into captivity are represented in equally up-to-date guise (p. 152 A). The old wars of the Bible and the latest war in defense of the Holy Land or the king's domain are part of a single history. Henry III in his bedchamber at Westminster could feast his eyes on the heroic deeds of the past, and see rude warfare formalized and sanctified.

**Gothic sentiment**

Of all the vanished masterpieces that decked the palaces of the English king, the one whose loss is perhaps most keenly to be regretted was the personification of Winter at Westminster. In 1240, King Henry ordered his painters to represent in the queen's chamber a figure "which by

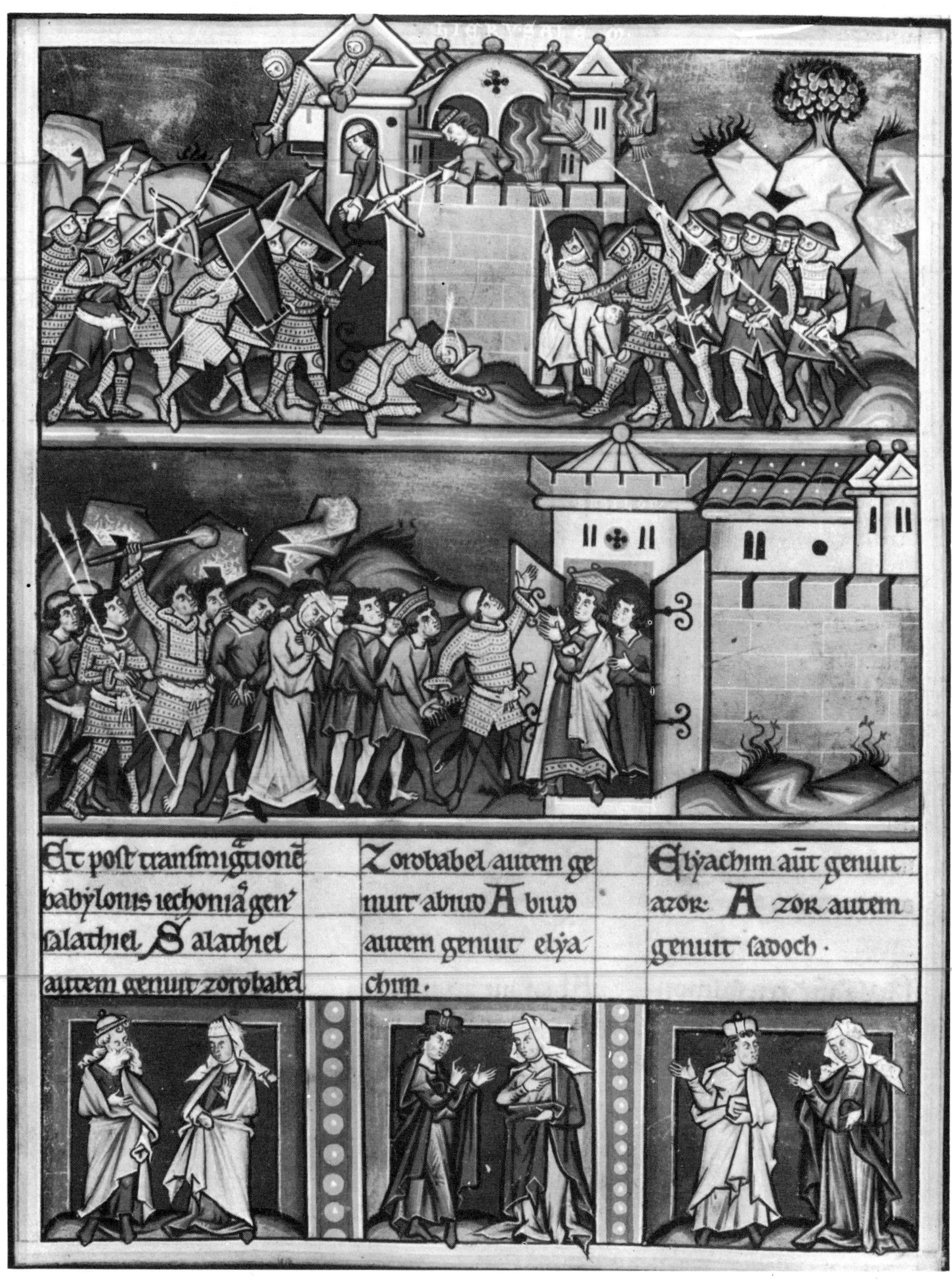
Et post transmigtionē
babylonis iechonias gen'
salathiel. Salathiel
autem genuit zorobabel
Zorobabel autem ge
nuit abiud. Abiud
autem genuit elya
chim.
Elyachim aūt genuit
azor. Azor autem
genuit sadoch.

A

its sad looks and other miserable portrayals of the body may be justly likened to Winter." There are skillful representations of "sad looks" both in the Good Samaritan window and de Brailes's psalter-page. The large-scale figure of Winter, painted for the delight of a queen with all the subtle care expected of a court artist, must have been a radiantly beautiful work. Such an evocation of a mood by means of gesture and the disposition of the body was quite beyond the powers of Romanesque artists, and would never have been demanded of them by their patrons. Gothic artists first learned to enlarge the scope of art in this way by absorbing the general religious atmosphere of their time. In the Gothic age, the Church carried its message to the people of Europe by emphasizing those aspects of the faith that appealed most strongly to the emotions, the helpless infancy of the God-Man and His sufferings for the salvation of mankind. Inevitably artists set themselves to express sentiments such as tenderness and pity, and to deepen the psychological and dramatic value of their art.

**Devotional imagery in Gothic art**

In his *Historia Anglorum*, Matthew Paris represented himself prostrate before the Virgin and uttering a rhapsodic prayer beginning "O blest kisses implanted by the Infant's lips!" Innumerable Gothic paintings bear witness to the popularity of the theme of the mutual love of Mary and the Christ-child (B). A painted roundel in the Bishop's palace at Chichester, executed with the elegant crispness characteristic of the court artists, shows the Virgin with crown and scepter seated on a splendid throne over which angels swing censers (p. 244). The Child stands on His mother's knees, looking fondly into her eyes and throwing His arms about her neck. The picture is at once ceremonial and charged with human feeling. Darker and more solemn emotions were equally within the range of the Gothic artist. The symbolic Crucifixion scene in a Regensburg manuscript, of about 1270, where the Saviour is nailed to the Cross by the Christian Virtues, presents Christ's death as a divine ritual, a sacred act of consent (p. 154 A). But in a miniature in a German psalter of about 1255, now at Melk, Christ mounts a ladder leaning against the cross and gazes at his persecutors with a look of weary reproach (p. 245). This image of the lonely Victim driven to his death by evil men marks the rebirth of pathos in European art.

(A) Bible history scenes: from Evangeliary, about 1260
*Aschaffenburg, Germany, Schlossbibl.* (MS. 13, f. 18v.)

(B) Lady de Quincy Adoring the Virgin and Child: from the Lambeth Apocalypse, about 1260
*London, Lambeth Palace Library* (MS. 209, f. 48)

(B) CIMABUE The Crucifixion (detail) about 1280
*Assisi, S. Francesco, Upper Church*

(A) The Crucifixion: from the Regensburg Legendary, about 1270
*Reproduced by permission of the Warden and Fellows of Keble College, Oxford*
(MS. 49, f. 7r.)

## Cimabue as wall painter

From pathos in Germany we move to the full tones of tragedy in Cimabue's great wall painting of *The Crucifixion*, of about 1280, in the Upper Church of St. Francis at Assisi (p. 246), part of a stupendous scheme of decoration that embraces the choir as well as both transepts, and includes scenes from the lives of saints and scenes from the Book of Revelation. Though "consumed by time and dust," to use the words of the 16th-century historian of Italian art, Giorgio Vasari, Cimabue's *Crucifixion* still retains its power to harrow and amaze. The swaying body of the Crucified recalls in its long curved limbs the sleeping Adam of the Chartres Good Samaritan window, and a detail like the priest grasping his beard (B) can be found in a late 13th-century French royal manuscript, the *Breviary of Philip the Fair*.

But the dramatic force and turbulence of the painting, not to speak of the scale, is beyond anything hinted at in the works of art so far considered. The quality of the work is such that only the most monumental of the French cathedral sculptures, those on the north transept façade at Reims, can rival it. No northern paintings survive that can do so. Gothic art came comparatively late to Italy, and mingled there with older but still powerful traditions. Cimabue's crucifix has something of the hieratic grandeur of Byzantine art, while the great crowd which surrounds the cross is handled with an authority born of a careful study of classical relief-sculpture.

(C) CIMABUE The Virgin and Child Enthroned, with Angels and Prophets:
(The Santa Trinità Madonna) about 1285
*Florence, Uffizi*

## Cimabue as panel painter

Cimabue's huge panel painting *The Virgin and Child Enthroned, with Angels and Prophets* from the Church of Santa Trinità in Florence is still Byzantine in the tight silhouette of the Virgin's head and the gold highlights of her cloak (C). On the other hand, the shaded multicolored wings and thin pliant draperies of the angels come close to those of the angel in the *Douce Apocalypse*, painted about 15 years earlier. The draperies also resemble those of the group of figures watching the annointing of David in the *Breviary of Philip the Fair* (D). Yet compared with these decorous and slightly affected northern paintings, Cimabue's panel achieves an unprecedented quality of heroic calm. It does so not only by its much larger scale, but by the convincing solidity of all the figures and especially of the magnificent throne. As the throne mounts up the panel it also recedes into depth, presenting many slanting surfaces to the eye. The angels standing behind and above each other also create a new illusion of reality. The Italian artist is breaking new ground, beyond the established limits of Gothic painting.

(D) The Anointing of David: from the Breviary of Philip the Fair, end of 13th century
*Paris, Bibliothèque Nationale*
(MS. Lat. 1023, f. 7v.)

A

B

## The term "Gothic"

In Italy the artists of the 15th-century Renaissance regarded themselves as the heirs of ancient Roman culture, and tried to recapture the qualities of Roman and Greek art (A, B). Judged by strictly classical standards, medieval art appeared naïve, unregulated, and essentially alien. Thus all the glorious post-classical monuments of Italy, paintings, mosaics, sculptures, and buildings, which expressed religious sentiments and aesthetic values outside the newly fashionable classical canon, were glibly attributed by 15th- and 16th-century critics and historians to the bad influence of ignorant foreigners, the Byzantine Greeks, the Germans, even absurdly the Goths, that long vanished race of barbarian invaders who helped to destroy the great political organism of the Roman Empire in the 3rd and 4th centuries.

When echoes of this kind of propagandist art history reached northern Europe in the 17th century they fell on welcoming ears. In Protestant lands, the Middle Ages were out of favor for religious reasons, and the term "Gothic," originally as forcibly derogatory as the term "vandal" is to this day, was adopted by scholars of the very nations whose genius had invented the condemned style. Gradually, medieval art has been recognized as no less beautiful, ingenious, and logical, along its own lines, than the classical style. As early as the 18th century, critics saw that medieval art exhibited many different stages of development, and new terms, notably "Romanesque," have lately been added to the original "Gothic." Through long custom, "Gothic" remains in use, though now confined to the style of art which emerged in France in the second half of the 12th century and which dominated all western Europe in the 13th century. By studying the vital and elegant works of French, English, German, and Italian "Gothic" painters, we can still enter into the spirit of the most mature and unruffled phase of western medieval civilization.

(A) Equestrian statue of Marcus Aurelius, about 173 A.D.
*Rome, Piazza del Campidoglio*

(B) DONATELLO Equestrian statue of Erasmo da Narni, called Gattamelata, 1443-53
*Padua*

(C) Saints and Prophets: from the west façade, about 1240
*Reims, Cathedral*

(D) The Descent from the Cross, 2nd half of the 13th century *ivory*
*Paris, Louvre*

C

*An elegant style of sculpture was developed in both large and small scale works. The great column figures of saints and prophets on the west facade of Reims Cathedral* (C) *were at one time decorated with paint. This kind of decoration can still be seen on the small but very striking ivory of the same period* (D).

D

*Sculptors working for great secular patrons were capable of producing works of great sophistication and psychological skill. A fine example is the head of a youth formerly set above a doorway in Henry III's palace at Clarendon, Wiltshire, England* (A).

*Examples of scientific naturalism in stone, depicting foliage or flowers on a large scale, are to be found in the great cathedrals of Europe* (B). *Further evidence of the precise and inquiring mind of artists of the period is found in similar naturalistic decorations, accurate in every detail, in medieval manuscripts.*

*The Nativity scene in Giovanni Pisano's pulpit at Pistoia* (C) *is crowded with figures and animals which give it a sense of strength and drama generally to be found in Italian sculpture.*

A

B

C

(A) Head of a Youth: from Henry III's Palace, Clarendon, Wiltshire, about 1240
*Salisbury, England, South Wiltshire and Blackmore Mus.*

(B) Capital from passage leading to the Chapter House, late 13th century
*Southwell, England, Minster*

(C) GIOVANNI PISANO The Nativity: detail from the pulpit, 1301
*Pistoia, Italy, S. Andrea*

D

*The great overseas wars of the Crusades dominated the imagination of medieval Europe and resulted in the creation of a truly international society and culture. Matthew Paris's lively drawing of an incident from the Crusades* (E) *is a form of contemporary journalism just as vivid, if not as accurate, as a modern newsreel.*

*Heraldry was the external symbolism of the military aristocracy of Europe. An example of heraldic art is the coats of arms of English and foreign notables carved on shields in the spandrels of the wall arcades of Westminster Abbey, London* (D).

(D) The Royal Arms of Henry III, about 1255
*London, Westminster Abbey*

(E) MATTHEW PARIS
The Capture of the Cross by Saladin, 1187: from "Chronica Majora," about 1250
*Cambridge, England, Corpus Christi College Library*
(MS. 26, f. 279)

E

*In literature, scholarship was still dominated by the Bible. A remarkable example of Biblical scholarship is the elaborately illustrated* Bible Moralisée *now at the Bodleian Library, Oxford* (A). *This is a great work expounding the meaning of the Bible in text and pictures, rather like a modern strip cartoon but with a lay-out reminiscent of a stained-glass window.*

*The scientific treatises of the period contained fantastic legendary material. Even in an authoritative book about animals like the* Ashmole Bestiary (B), *all sorts of strange creatures are illustrated and described in the text.*

A

B

(A) "Bible Moralisée," 1st half of the 13th century
*Oxford, Bodleian Library* (MS. Bodl. 270 B, f. 55v.)

(B) The Capture of the Unicorn: from the Ashmole Bestiary, about 1200
*Oxford, Bodleian Library* (Ashmole MS. 1511, f. 14v.)

C

D

(C) Tristram and Yseult on a Bench; and Tristram and Yseult in the Love Grotto: from "Roman de la Poire," about 1260
*Paris, Bibl. Nat.* (MS. 2186, f. 5v.)

(D) The Coronation of the Virgin, about 1260 *ivory*
*Paris, Louvre*

*However, secular literature also abounded, notably in the courtly romances of King Arthur and his companions. Artists turned easily from depicting religious subjects to illustrating these romances. Tristram and Yseult sitting on a bench* (C) *adopt the same attitude as the two figures of the ivory carving in* The Coronation of the Virgin (D). *The lay-out of the page again has a strong resemblance to a stained-glass window.*

B

A

C

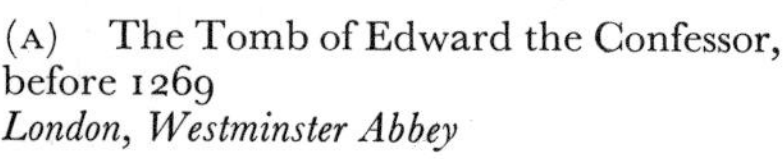

(A) The Tomb of Edward the Confessor, before 1269
*London, Westminster Abbey*

(B) The Tomb of Edward the Confessor (detail) before 1269
*London, Westminster Abbey*

(C) AMBROGIO LORENZETTI Peace and Fortitude: from the Allegory of Good Government, 1337-40
*Siena, Palazzo Pubblico*

*Italian artists traveled all over Europe and their styles were adopted in the north. The tomb of Edward the Confessor in Westminster Abbey, London* (A) *is by an Italian artist who signed his work " Petrus, Romanus Civis. " The tomb has mosaic inlay and twisted marble columns in the Italian manner* (B).

*Italian secular painting of the 14th century shows us what the lost secular paintings in France and England must have looked like. We may get some idea of the allegorical figures like the* Winter, *commissioned by Henry III, from the figure of* Peace *in Ambrogio Lorenzetti's* Allegory of Good Government (C).

*Gothic architecture in Northern Europe did not allow for wall painting inside churches. The vaulting ribs and wall shafts in cathedrals such as at Amiens, France* (D) *did not leave any room for paintings. The end walls of the nave and transepts usually contained a great display of stained glass such as at Chartres* (*p. 164* A). *Italian Gothic architecture, on the other hand, is more conservative; the windows are kept small, leaving plenty of scope for wall paintings* (*p. 164* B).

(D) The nave, 1st half of 13th century
*Amiens, France, Cathedral*

(A) South transept rose and lancet windows, 1st half of 13th century
*Chartres, France, Notre Dame Cathedral*

(B) Interior, 1253
*Assisi, S. Francesco, Upper Church*

A

B

*In the Gothic period, much Classical artistic tradition, literature, and history was incomprehensible; the relics of antiquity were interpreted in a thoroughly medieval way.*

*Villard de Honnecourt, the French architect and draftsman of the 13th century, sketched a tomb monument which, although Roman, he attributed to a Saracen; that is to say, he brought it up to date* (C).

*The Treasury of St. Albans Abbey, England, contained a huge late 4th-century cameo depicting the emperor holding the rod and serpent of the god of medicine, Aesculapius, and a Victory, and with the Imperial Eagle at his feet. Matthew Paris drew the cameo* (D) *and interpreted it in a medieval manner; he called it "Kaadmau" and said it was beneficial to women in childbirth.*

*Classical allusions in art remained fashionable, as is seen in the profile head imitating a classical cameo on the frame of the Westminster Retable in Westminster Abbey, London* (E).

*In the same way, classical heroes were put into a context which could generally be understood at the time. Alexander the Great not only becomes a medieval king but also a powerful magician. In the "Romance of Alexander" he is shown descending into the sea in a submarine made of glass and iron. The story of Alexander was also painted on walls at Clarendon Palace in about 1230 and at Nottingham Castle in about 1252.*

C

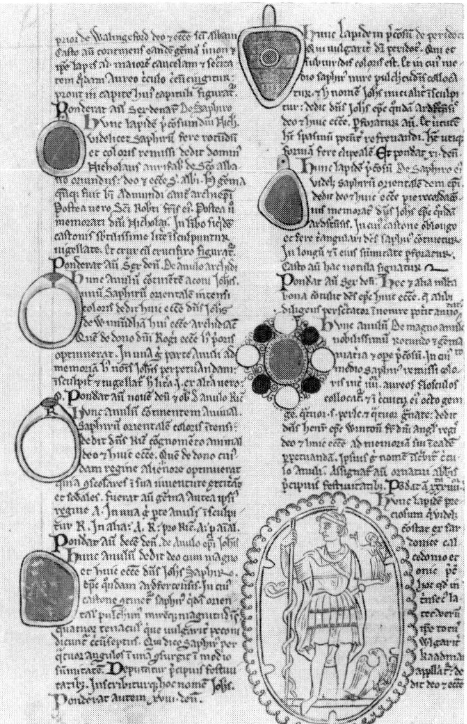

D

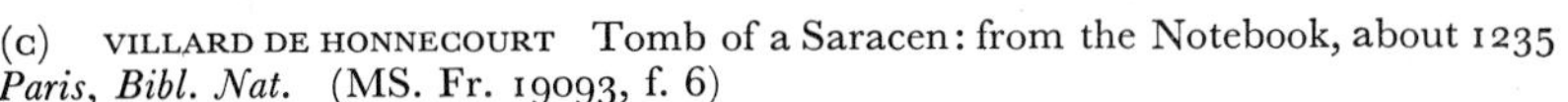

(C) VILLARD DE HONNECOURT Tomb of a Saracen: from the Notebook, about 1235
*Paris, Bibl. Nat.* (MS. Fr. 19093, f. 6)

(D) MATTHEW PARIS Drawing of a cameo: from Description of the Treasury of St. Albans Abbey, mid-13th century
*London, B. M.* (MS. Cotton Nero D. i., f. 146)

(E) Profile from the frame of the Westminster Retable, 1260-70 *1 in. across*
*London, Westminster Abbey*

E

# Color Plates

First Style Architectural Wall: from the Samnite House, Herculaneum, 2nd century B. C. *wall painting*
*Naples, Museo Nazionale*

Second Style Architectural Wall: from the Villa of the Mysteries, Pompeii, 1st century B. C. *wall painting*
*Naples, Museo Nazionale*

The Landing of Odysseus: from the Odyssey Landscapes, 1st century B. C. *wall painting*
*Rome, Vatican Library*

Wall painting from Nero's Golden House, 1st century A. D.
*Rome, Museo Nazionale*

Frieze of the Dionysiac Mysteries (detail): from the Villa of the Mysteries, Pompeii, 1st century B.C. *wall painting height 64 in.*
*Pompeii, Villa dei Misteri*

Scene of the Triclinium: from the House of the Fruit Orchard, Pompeii, 1st century B.C. *wall painting*
*Pompeii, Casa degli Orti*

Perseus Freeing Andromeda: from the House of Dioscurides, Pompeii *wall painting transferred to panel 48 × 39½ in. Naples, Museo Nazionale*

The Garden Room: from the Villa of Livia, Prima Porta, Rome, 1st century B. C. / 1st century A. D. *wall painting height 118 in.*
*Rome, Museo Nazionale*

Still-life with Eggs and Game: from the House of Julia Felix, Pompeii, 1st century B. C. / 1st century A. D. *wall painting transferred to panel*
*Naples, Museo Nazionale*

The Alexander Mosaic: from the House of the Faun, Pompeii, about 90 B. C. *mosaic* $106\frac{3}{4} \times 201\frac{5}{8}$ *in.*
*Naples, Museo Nazionale*

Portrait of Constantine and Wine Harvest, mid-4th century A. D. *ambulatory ceiling mosaic*
*Rome, S. Costanza*

Wall decorations, mid-2nd century A. D. *fresco*
*Rome, Domitilla Catacomb, Flavii Hypogeum*

The Breaking of Bread, early 3rd century A. D. *fresco*
*Rome, Priscilla Catacomb, Cappella Greca*

The Arenarium Madonna and Child, first half of the 3rd century A. D. *fresco*
*Rome, Priscilla Catacomb*

Detail of Priests: from The Sacrifice of Conon, late 1st / early 2nd century A. D.
(from: "Oriental Forerunners of Byzantine Painting" by J. H. Breasted) *fresco*
*Dura Europos, Syria, Temple of Palmyrene Gods*

Orants in the Garden of Paradise, end of the 3rd century A. D. *fresco*
*Rome, Callixtus Catacomb, Five Saints Crypt*

Orant, about 330 A. D. *wall painting*
*Rome, Trasone Catacomb, Coemiterium Maius*

Christ Enthroned amidst His Apostles, early 5th century *apse mosaic*
*Rome, S. Pudenziana*

St. Lawrence, second half of the 5th century *mosaic*
*Ravenna, Mausoleum of Galla Placidia*

Altar with the Gospel of St. John, third quarter of the 5th century *mosaic*
*Ravenna, Baptistery of the Orthodox*

Symbolic Throne, early 6th century *mosaic*
*Ravenna, Baptistery of the Arians*

Angel: Symbol of the Evangelist St. Matthew, late 5th - early 6th century *mosaic*
*Ravenna, Archbishop's Palace*

Procession of Saints (detail) about 560 *mosaic*
*Ravenna, S. Apollinare Nuovo*

Christ Surrounded by Saints, about 530 *apse mosaic*
*Rome, S. Cosma e S. Damiano*

Theodora and her Courtiers (detail) mid-6th century *mosaic*
*Ravenna, S. Vitale*

The Transfiguration of Christ and St. Apollinare, mid-6th century *apse mosaic*
*Ravenna, S. Apollinare in Classe*

Architectural Landscape with Martyrs, early 5th century *dome mosaic*
*Salonika, Greece, Church of St. George*

Three Saints, 11th century *icon*
*Mount Sinai, Egypt, Monastery of St. Catherine*

Patron Saint and Founders, 6th-7th century *mosaic*
*Salonika, Greece, Church of St. Demetrius*

Moses and the Israelites: from the Paris Psalter, 10th century *vellum*
*Paris, Bibliothèque Nationale* (MS. Grec. 139)

The Prophets David and Solomon: from The Descent into Hell, 1042-56 *mosaic*
*Chios, Monastery of Nea Moni*

The Annunciation, 11th century *mosaic*
*Daphni, near Athens, Church of the Dormition*

The Virgin and Child, early 11th century *apse mosaic*
*Torcello, Italy, Cathedral*

Christ Pantocrator, about 1150 *apse mosaic*
*Cefalù, Sicily, Cathedral*

Our Lady of Vladimir, about 1125 *icon* $39\frac{1}{4} \times 27\frac{1}{2}$ *in.* (*including frame*)
*Moscow, Tretyakov Gallery*

Deësis Panel: Christ between the Virgin and St. John the Baptist, 12th or 13th century *mosaic*
*Istanbul, Sancta Sophia*

Jacob's Struggle with the Angel, about 1260 *wall painting*
*Trebizond, Turkey, Sancta Sophia*
*By courtesy of the Russell Trust Expedition*

The Betrayal of Christ, 1230-37 *wall painting*
*Mileševa, Yugoslavia, Monastery*

The Dormition of the Virgin (detail) about 1350 *wall painting*
*Mistra, Greece, Church of the Perebleptos*

The Nativity, 1428 *wall painting*
*Mistra, Greece, Church of the Pantanassa*

Sarah, Genesis XVI, 5; and Lot Defends his Home against the Sodomites, Genesis XIX, 11: from the Cotton Genesis, late 4th century A. D. *vellum*
*London, British Museum*

Portrait of St. Luke: from the St. Augustine's Gospels, late 6th century *vellum 8 × 6½ in.*
*Cambridge, England, Corpus Christi College Library* (MS. 286, f. 129v.)

Scenes from the story of Lot; and the story of Abraham: from the Ashburnham Pentateuch, 7th century
*vellum* $14\frac{1}{2} \times 12\frac{1}{2}$ *in.*
*Paris, Bibliothèque Nationale* (MS. Lat. 2334, f. 18r.)

Portrait of St. Matthew: from the Book of Durrow, f. 21v., second half of the 7th century
*vellum* $9\frac{5}{8} \times 6\frac{1}{8}$ *in.*
*By permission of the Board of Trinity College, Dublin*

Beginning of St. Matthew Gospel: from the Lindisfarne Gospels, early 8th century
*vellum* $13\frac{1}{2} \times 9\frac{3}{4}$ *in.*
*London, British Museum* (MS. Cotton Nero D. IV, f. 29r.)

Christ Enthroned: from the Godescalc Gospels, 781-783 *vellum* $12 \times 8\frac{1}{4}$ *in.*
*Paris, Bibliothèque Nationale* (Nouv. Acq. Lat. 1203, f. 3r.)

Portrait of St. Matthew, early 9th century *vellum*
*London, British Museum* (MS. Harley 2788, f. 13v.)

Portrait of St. Luke: from the Ebbo Gospels, 816-833 *vellum* $10\frac{1}{4} \times 8$ *in.*
*Épernay, France, Bibliothèque Municipale* (MS. 1, f. 90v.)

The Baptism of Christ: from the Benediction of St. Ethelwold, about 980 *vellum* $9\frac{7}{8} \times 7\frac{7}{8}$ *in.*
*London, British Museum* (MS. Add. 49598, f. 25)

Portrait of St. John: from the Grimbald Gospels, early 11th century *vellum* $12\frac{3}{4} \times 9\frac{3}{4}$ *in.*
*London, British Museum* (MS. Add. 34890, f. 114v.)

The Healing of the Blind Man: from the Egbert Codex, about 980 *vellum* $4\times5\frac{1}{4}$ *in.*
*Trier, Germany, Stadtbibliothek* (Cod. 24, f. 50r.)

The Emperor Enthroned: from the Otto III Gospels, about 1000 *vellum*
*Munich, Bayerische Staatsbibliothek* (Cod. Lat. 4453, f. 24r.)

The Annunciation to the Shepherds: from the Henry II Gospels, about 1007-12 *vellum 11 × 8¼ in.*
*Munich, Bayerische Staatsbibliothek* (Cod. Lat. 4452, f. 8v.)

Storm on the Sea of Galilee: from the Hitda Gospels, early 11th century *vellum* $6\frac{5}{8} \times 4\frac{5}{8}$ *in.*
*Darmstadt, Germany, Landesbibliothek* (Cod. 1640, f. 117)

The Parable of the Marriage Supper: from Henry III's Codex Aureus, mid-11th century *vellum*
*Madrid, The Escorial Library* (Codex Vitrinas 17, f. 115r.)

Christ in Majesty, 11th century *apse fresco*
*Near Capua, Italy, Abbey Church of S. Angelo in Formis*

The Last Judgment (detail of angel) 11th century *fresco*
*Near Capua, Italy, Abbey Church of S. Angelo in Formis*

The Archangel Michael and the Prophet Jeremiah, 1007 *fresco*
*Galliano, Italy, Basilica of S. Vincenzo*

The Ark on the Waters: from the History of Noah, about 1100 *fresco*
*Saint-Savin-sur-Gartempe, France, Abbey Church*

Christ in Majesty, 12th century *wall painting*
*Berzé-la-Ville, France, Cluniac Priory*

St. Paul and the Viper, about 1150 *fresco 69×66 in.*
*Canterbury, England, Cathedral, Chapel of St. Anselm*

The Crucifixion: from the Winchester Psalter, about 1070 *vellum* $12 \times 7\frac{1}{2}$ *in.*
*London, British Museum* (MS. Arundel 60, f. 52v.)

Illustrations to the Book of Deuteronomy: from the Bury Bible, about 1145
*vellum* $20\frac{1}{2} \times 14$ *in.*
*Cambridge, England, Corpus Christi College Library* (MS. 2, f. 94r.)

Illuminated Initial: from the Winchester Bible, f. 34v., late 12th century *vellum* $5 \times 5\frac{3}{4}$ *in.* (*initial only*)
*Winchester, England, Cathedral Library*
*By permission of the Dean and Chapter of Winchester*

The Visitation: from the Westminster Psalter, about 1200
*vellum 9 × 6¼ in.*
*London, British Museum* (MS. Royal 2, A. XXII)

Illuminated Initial: from "The Life of St. Martial of Limoges," by Pseudo-Aurelianus, 11th century
*vellum* $13\frac{3}{4} \times 8\frac{1}{4}$ *in.*
*Paris, Bibliothèque Nationale* (MS. Lat. 5296A, f. 2v.)

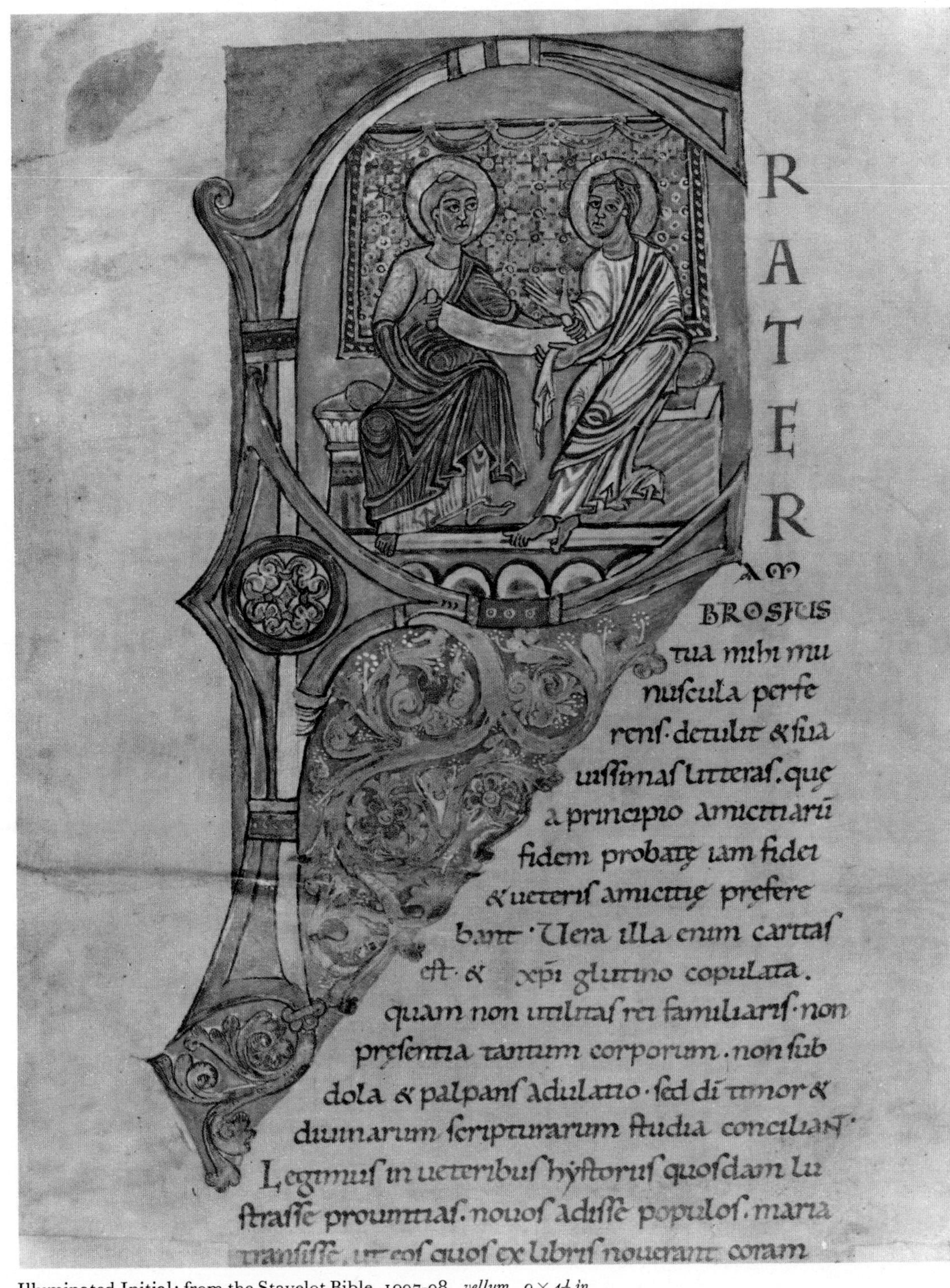


Illuminated Initial: from the Stavelot Bible, 1097-98 *vellum* $9 \times 4\frac{1}{4}$ *in.*
*London, British Museum* (MS. Add. 28106, f. 2v.)

The Pentecost, and the Agony in the Garden: from the Ingeborg Psalter, about 1200 *vellum*
*Chantilly, France, Musée Condé* (MS. Add. 1695, f. 24v. and 32v.)

Enoch, window in south transept, 12th century *stained glass*
*Canterbury, England, Cathedral*

The Good Samaritan Window (detail) early 13th century *stained glass*
*Chartres, France, Notre Dame Cathedral*

W. DE BRAILES Six incidents from the stories of Adam and Eve, Cain, and Lamech, 1st half of the 13th century *vellum* $9\frac{7}{8} \times 6\frac{7}{8}$ *in.*
*Cambridge, England, Fitzwilliam Museum* (MS. 330)

Samson and the Lion; and Samson with the Gates of Gaza: from the St. Louis Psalter, early 13th century *vellum*
*Leiden, Holland, University Library* (MS. 76A)

MATTHEW PARIS Drawing of an Elephant: from "Chronica Majora," 1255 *tinted drawing on vellum* $14\frac{1}{4}\times9\frac{5}{8}$ *in.*
*Cambridge, England, Corpus Christi College Library* (MS. 16, f. 151b.)

Angel Blowing Trumpet: from the Douce Apocalypse, about 1270 *vellum* $4\frac{1}{2}\times5\frac{3}{4}$ *in.*
*Oxford, Bodleian Library* (MS. Douce 180, p. 26)

Joseph Revealing himself to his Brothers: from the St. Louis Psalter, 1253-70 *vellum*
*Paris, Bibliothèque Nationale* (MS. Lat. 10525, f. 25v.)

St. Peter: detail from the Westminster Retable, 1260-70 *tempera on panel* *about 24 × 19 in.*
*London, Westminster Abbey*

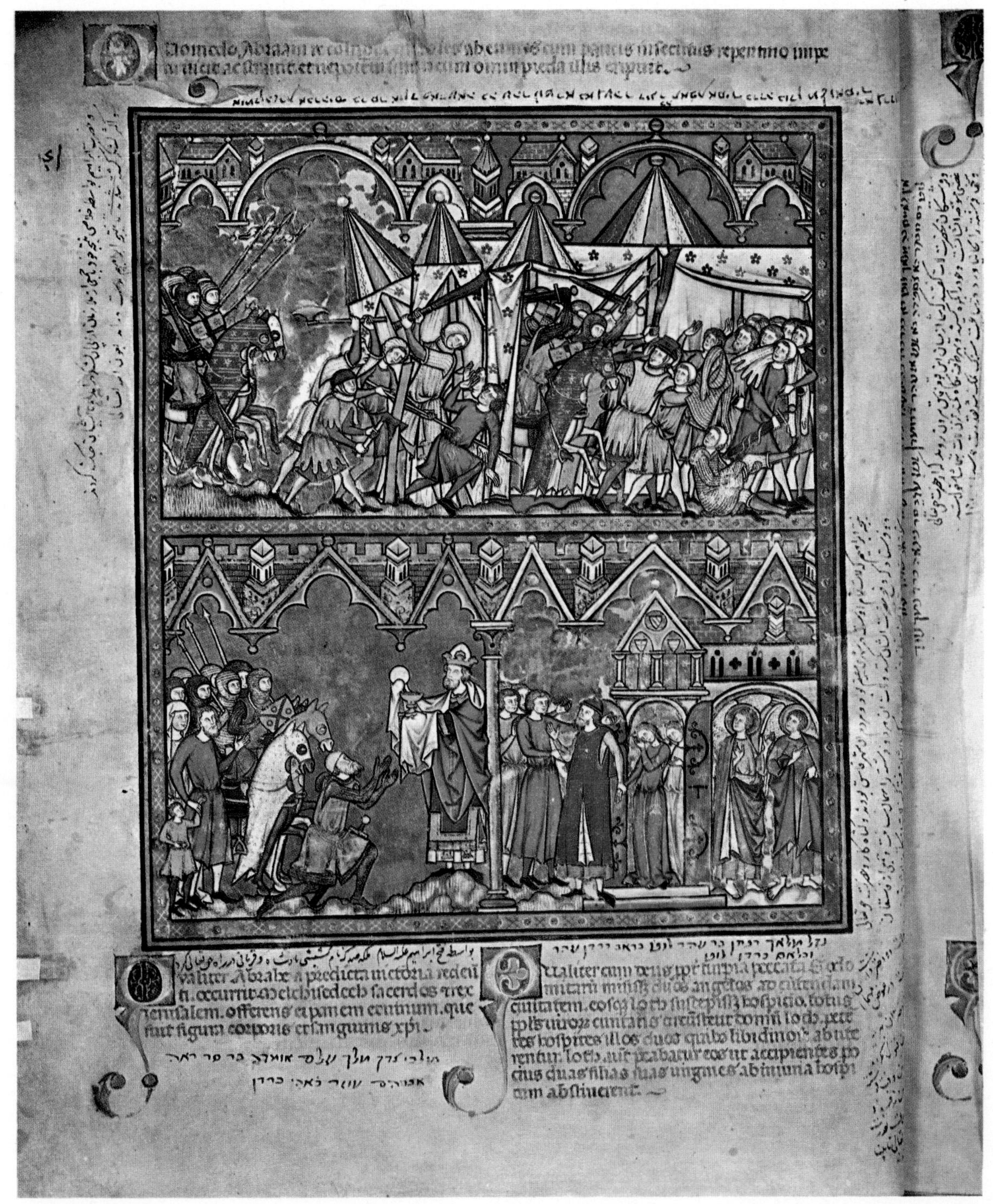

Abraham's Rout of the King of Elam; Abraham and Melchizedek; and Lot at Sodom: from the Maciejowski Bible, about 1250 *vellum*
*New York, J. Pierpont Morgan Library* (MS. 638, f. 3v.)

The Virgin and Child Adored by Angels: the Chichester Roundel, about 1250 *wall painting diameter 32 in.*
*Chichester, England, Chapel of the Bishop's Palace*

Christ Ascending the Cross: from the Psalter of Bamberg, about 1255 *vellum*
*Melk, Austria, Stiftsbibliothek* (Eichstätter Diocese MS. 1833, f. 47v.)

CIMABUE The Crucifixion, about 1280 *fresco*
*Assisi, S. Francesco, Upper Church*

## THE VOLUMES

1 ORIGINS OF WESTERN ART
General Introduction by Sir Herbert Read
Contributors: Donald E. Strong, Professor Giuseppe Bovini, David Talbot Rice, Peter Lasko, Dr. George Henderson, Professor George Zarnecki

2 ITALIAN ART TO 1850
Edited by Professor Mario Monteverdi, *Professor of History of Art, Liceo Classico Manzoni, Milan*

3 FLEMISH AND DUTCH ART
Edited by Professor A. M. Hammacher, *Former Director, Rijksmuseum, Kröller-Müller, Otterlo*
and Dr. R. Hammacher Vandenbrande, *Boymans-van Beuningen Museum, Rotterdam*

4 GERMAN AND SPANISH ART TO 1900
Edited by Dr. Horst Vey, *Wallraf-Richartz-Museum, Cologne*
and Dr. Xavier de Salas, *Deputy Director, Museo del Prado, Madrid*

5 FRENCH ART FROM 1350 TO 1850
Edited by Michel Laclotte, *Principal Inspector of Provincial Museums, France*

6 BRITISH AND NORTH AMERICAN ART TO 1900
Edited by Dr. Kenneth Garlick, *Lecturer in History of Art and Deputy Director, Barber Institute of Fine Arts, Birmingham*

7 IMPRESSIONISTS AND POST-IMPRESSIONISTS
Edited by Alan Bowness, *Lecturer, Courtauld Institute of Art, University of London*

8 MODERN ART
Edited by David Sylvester

9 CHINESE AND JAPANESE ART
By Dr. Michael Sullivan, *Lecturer in Asian Art, School of Oriental and African Studies, University of London*

10 HOW TO LOOK AT ART
By Bernard Myers, *Lecturer, Royal College of Art, London*